Praise for the Author

"I started seeing Jacqui because I was at a crossroads in life, needing some direction and help making a decision about what I wanted to do. Jacqui's understanding of my situation really helped me to break things down and realise I was much more capable than I gave myself credit for. Jacqui helped bring me inner clarity, self-confidence and the ability to believe in myself."

A.T

"I felt calmer and less confused after a consultation with Jacqui, and learnt that I can only change myself and not other people. Jacqui was able to validate me and gave me ideas about how to deal with conflict. I learnt how understanding and changing my reactions to others changed how they responded toward me."

W.M

"Jacqui showed me how down I had become within my marriage and how unhappy that had made me. With one session Jacqui made me realise that it is okay to speak up. I remember very well the feeling of enlightenment, when I went back and told her about the new me and how she had given me the strength to take back control of my life. Jacqui has an uncanny ability to be able to read people and with her intuition can sum things up very quickly. I felt at ease straight away when we met and developed a rapport very quickly."

G.R

"My first sessions with Jacqui were after being in a serious car accident. I was embarking on a separation from my husband at the same time and Jacqui provided strategies to help manage the separation. I needed to deal with the fallout from the ending of a long marriage in which children were involved. Jacqui's warmth and professionalism gave me the support and confidence I needed to be able to manage all that I had to do."

E.Q

"I could write a novel on the ways Jacqui has helped me. Before every session I became anxious, reluctant and scared at the thought of opening myself up and being so vulnerable. The moment I began a conversation with Jacqui, I felt immediately calmed, relaxed and as open as I could possibly be. It was as though the previous thought demons didn't even exist. It's a great trait that only a few really hold."

J.G

"After my sessions with Jacqui I feel almost indestructible, the light switch is on and I greet the world with the most open heart and mind and the kind of positivity that has only been sourced out from one magnificent kind of human being. Jacqui Christie, thank you!"

G.J

"Jacqui has been a huge help for my relationship, helping me to understand myself and my partner from a different perspective has helped resolve conflicts. After my sessions with Jacqui, I always have a sense of relief, clarity of thought and an improved confidence I can handle life ups and downs."

A.T

"Jacqui has a gift of creating a safe space to explore problems and unravel what can seem like an impossibly complex knot of issues and feelings. Jacqui guides you to find the individual threads, so they become clear and workable. She has a way of transforming a person's perception from 'this is impossible' to 'I am capable to do this'."

L.M

"Jacqui has had such a positive impact on my life. Prior to working with her I was incredibly stressed and with that came anxiety, but from the very first meeting Jacqui showed such empathy and I felt she truly listened to me. Jacqui has a real talent of understanding, showing empathy and at the same time, gently challenging you when the need arises. I really value her honesty. She has provided me with many practical strategies and they have worked every time. When I realised that I was holding back on having some important conversations Jacqui helped me to structure those and have the courage to speak with those concerned. It has been a very positive experience. Jacqui has a wealth of knowledge and experience and I am truly grateful for her assistance and advice."

T.H

"We first came to see Jacqui as we were unsure if we should stay together. Through Jacqui's help we have learnt how to communicate in a more loving and understanding way. We have begun the journey of healing our relationship after many years of us both feeling alone. We are now able to listen to each other's points of view and feel more trusting of each other."

B.P

Rewire Your Relationship™

Global Publishing Group
Australia • New Zealand • Singapore • America • London

Rewire Your Relationship™

A PRACTICAL GUIDE TO CREATING A LOVING AND PASSIONATE RELATIONSHIP

JACQUI CHRISTIE

DISCLAIMER

All the information, techniques, skills and concepts contained within this publication are of the nature of general comment only and are not in any way recommended as individual advice. The intent is to offer a variety of information to provide a wider range of choices now and in the future, recognising that we all have widely diverse circumstances and viewpoints. Should any reader choose to make use of the information contained herein, this is their decision, and the contributors (and their companies), authors and publishers do not assume any responsibilities whatsoever under any condition or circumstances. It is recommended that the reader obtain their own independent advice.

First Edition 2017

National Library of Australia

Cataloguing-in-Publication entry:

Creator: Christie, Jacqui, author.

Title: Rewire Your Relationship : A Practical Guide to Creating a Loving and Passionate Relationship / Jacqui Christie.

ISBN: 9781925288124 (paperback)

Subjects: Man-woman relationships.
Interpersonal relations.
Relationship quality.

Published by Global Publishing Group
PO Box 517 Mt Evelyn, Victoria 3796 Australia
Email info@GlobalPublishingGroup.com.au

Editing by: Alex Mitchell, www.AuthorSupportServices.com

For further information about orders:
Phone: +61 3 9739 4686 or Fax +61 3 8648 6871

I dedicate this book to my father Peter Simpson Christie
who continued his quest for learning and self-development
till the day he left this earth and who encouraged me
on the same quest.

Acknowledgements

To my husband Peter who has been a tireless support for me throughout our relationship and can truly 'see' and accept me, warts and all. Without you I would not have been able to achieve any of the goals I have in our life together.

To my parents, Pat and Pete, for raising me to believe I can achieve anything I set my mind to. For having the opportunity to experience living in different cultures at such a young age, which not only expanded my horizons but my viewpoint on the world. Without those seminal experiences, I would not have developed into who I am today. To my sister Donna – we have both been on an amazing journey throughout our lives. Thank you for having always believed in me and having faith in my ability to show who I truly am.

Gratitude to my son Lyndon who has one of my greatest fans throughout my journey of learning and development cheering me on with every goal I have set. And to my beautiful daughter Ashley who has inspired me to continue on by her own tireless efforts in attaining her goals and balancing work, play and study at such a young age.

To my dearest friends who have helped keep my sanity, challenged and supported me through my own life. Daphne, my oldest friend, who is always in my heart even though we are on other sides of the world. Linda, who encouraged, guided

and inspired me to develop into an empowered woman. To Ange, who reminded me just how important my relationship was and to spend the time nurturing it.

To Irma who was a rock solid absolute support for me when I began my journey of learning and psychology. To my beautiful friends, Giovanna and Nikki who I trust implicitly that I can reach out to at any time and are always there for me.

To all the clients and couples that have taken the courageous step to allow me into their lives and share themselves open-heartedly. Not only have I learnt from you about how relationships function but you have given me the inspiration and motivation to develop a greater understanding of my own relationship and how we as humans connect to each other.

I would like to thank the many teachers and mentors who have influenced guided and inspired me to believe in myself and to reach my full potential. Special mentions are my Nanny who was my first mentor, Mrs Wright my Year 10 tutor, Lorna Hoess, Harville Hendrix, Dr Daniella Guidara, Dr John Demartini, Luanne Simmons and Dr Karen Weiss.

To the amazingly grounded and talented Dr Stan Tatkin who through his teaching gave me the confidence and inspiration to write this book.

I must thank Alex Mitchell, my editor at Author Support Services, for her patience, commitment and just going above and beyond to help me write this book.

Last but by no means least a special thank you goes to Darren J Stephens, his beautiful wife Jackie Tallentyre and the team at Global Publishing, without whom this book would not have been completed. They have been my behind the scenes cheer squad, and reminded me that it's never too late to put your hand up.

I cannot give you everything
you need about creating a connected and fulfilling
relationship in one small book.

So I've created some extra special goodies just for you.

You'll find special offers for upcoming workshops and retreats that will help fast-track your relationship transformation. Just like my...

Heart Tips
For Keeping Your Relationship On Track

Go and check out it out now,
it's all free at

www.RewireYouRelationship.com/bonus

Contents

Preface

If you think about it, everything is relationships, from the way you greet your café owner in the morning to how you end the day with your partner. It is all an interaction, a dynamic, a relationship. So it makes sense to be who you really are in your relationships. Especially your most intimate relationship, the one that matters to you the most.

Relationships for me are at the heart of everything. There is nothing more important to me than relationships, including my own. This is why I have spent my entire life understanding, working on and helping other people to understand their relationships.

As a young child I was interested in listening to people's stories, especially their history and how that led to who they became. I loved sitting and listening to my Nanny talk about her life and family when she was young and would ask her endless questions about the meaning of life. Why, why and why. No question was too difficult for her as she always seemed to have an answer for me.

As I grew up my interest in family stories turned to questions about why one person's life went down one path and another person's life went down another.

The curiosity I had in people and their lives led me to the study of human behaviour at university, which led me onto becoming a psychologist. In those days, my interest was on power and inequality with men and women, and my original career choice was forensic psychology. Understanding the elements of power and control and how this behaviour manifested in relationships was a primary focus. I worked for over a decade in the field of family violence, initially working with men and later women, to enable change.

My work with couples developed from here. Couples therapy is very different to therapy with an individual, because of the different dynamic and energy created between couples who are in a relationship. I found the work interesting, challenging and exciting and wanted to learn more about the different ways that couples could strengthen their relationships.

I met the wonderful Dr Stan Tatkin and decided to study his newly developed Psychobiological Approach to Couples Therapy (PACT). During an introductory workshop, I discovered that learning this cutting-edge approach of neurobiological research, blended with arousal and attachment theory, was something I just had to do. Not only was this a completely revolutionary approach to couples therapy, but it deeply resonated with me and with what I had previously learned. What I didn't realise at this point was just how much of our early experiences are *HARD WIRED* in our brains. PACT gave me the framework through which I could express my ideas about relationships and was a turning point in my career as a therapist. I became passionate about adult attachment and how our early development impacts each and every one of us every day of our lives.

I came to realise that my life purpose has been to guide, mentor and counsel men and women in different areas of their lives but especially in their relationships. It is something I have been doing my entire life in different ways.

Through the encouragement of others, I became aware that writing a book was a vital avenue for me to be able to support even more relationships, marriages and partnerships. I wanted to pass on some of my knowledge, learning and wisdom in human behaviour hopefully to enable change in other people's lives.

As my reader, you are here to learn more about relationships and how to create a long-lasting relationship for yourself. Perhaps you want to deepen the connection that you already have with your current partner. My wish for you is that in reading this book you will become empowered to think differently about yourself and the people who mean the most to you in your life. That knowledge and understanding will flow into creating a safe and secure and loving relationship for the both of you.

Introduction

Every day I sit with clients just like you who are struggling in their relationships. People who are at their wits end with each other, from the couple who are constantly arguing to the couple who are hardly talking to each other at all. People tell me how their heart tells them one thing and their head another, and they don't know what to believe anymore. Their partner is on a different wavelength to them and does not understand them or what they need. They tell me how they don't trust their partner or their partner does not trust them. And some couples of course are teetering on the edge of separation.

It's harder than ever these days to stay in a relationship and make it work. In our society everything seems to take precedence over intimate relationships. There are so many things competing for your attention, sometimes, it may seem easier to work on the parts of life that come more naturally to you like caring for the children or climbing the heights of your career.

It has been found that much of the success in intimate relating comes down to attachment. Attachment is one of the broadest and most complex topics in modern psychology, generating countless scientific papers and books. Historically, studies have focussed on infant attachment but more recently researchers have become interested in how attachment influences who you are throughout your life. This is called Adult Attachment.

In these pages I will be referring to the hallmark work on attachment theory by experts John Bowlby, Mary Ainsworth, Diane Poole Heller, Mario Mikulincer, Allan Schore, Marion Solomon, Rachel Heller, Amir Levine, and Stan Tatkin. Their research, and that of so many others in this field, has shown us amazing new understandings of the emotional and neurobiological origins of attachment styles. This understanding, together with the revelations of brain plasticity, gives us the opportunity to change lifelong destructive relationship patterns. We can now more than ever create positive behaviours that lead to deeper, more connected and longer lasting adult relationships.

Your attachment patterns were created from the moment you were born, and continue to affect the way you communicate with your partner and how you respond when conflict arises. For over 22 years my work with couples and individuals has been to distil this research down to real life strategies for real people in real relationships.

The pain you are feeling right now can be understood and managed through understanding your attachment styles. Through this framework you can begin to see your partner and yourself through new eyes.

Through these pages, I hope to help you understand why you behave the way you do in your relationship and give you some practical suggestions to manage things differently.

About the book

As this book is a self-help book to assist you in your current relationship it is designed with the two of you in mind. That being said if only one of you reads it there are still a large number of ideas, tips and techniques that will help you begin to understand your relationship from a different viewpoint.

Throughout the book I refer to the term *primary caregiver, caregiver and primary*. These terms are interchangeable and refer to the same person. Most often it will be your mother but this is not always the case as there are many people who were raised by other people in their life, family or otherwise.

To get the best out of this book I suggest you read it cover to cover as each chapter builds on the next. The book is in six parts. Each part has a specific focus on different aspects of your relationship and is designed so you can easily and quickly find some motivation, explanation or insight into what is happening in your relationship right now.

If you are looking for relationship inspiration you can flick through to find the Heart Tips which you can begin to implement to improve your relationship right now.

From understanding how your attachment style is developed and how it is directing every part of your life, to learning how to play with your partner and have fun, to increasing your intimacy and passion together – in this book I have attempted to cover the topics most requested from the couples I have worked with. There are also a number of tools, techniques and exercises that you can implement straight away with your partner for an immediate relationship benefit.

PART ONE

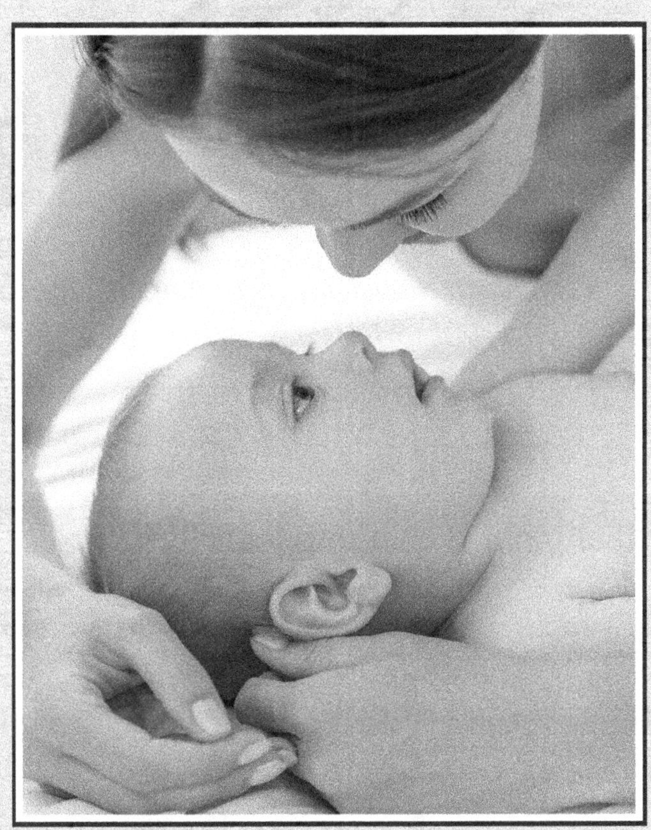

Your Brain and Attachment

PART ONE

Your Brain and Attachment

"The relationship you are born into is your very first relationship and sets the tone for all the relationships you have in your life."

– Jacqui Christie

How attachment is steering your life

Your early neurobiological development is impacting on your current relationships. In other words, how your brain developed as a baby is continuing to play a part in your relationships right now.

How does your early brain development become the template for every relationship you have?

When you were born, you were *not* born into an empty space. You had someone to care for you. I'll let that settle for a minute so you can think about what I just said. You had someone there on hand to care for you. That person was your

mother, father, another family member or someone outside of your family, and is called your primary caregiver. Your primary caregiver is the main person who took care of you. You began to respond to your primary caregiver and they began to respond back to you, and back and forth until what is created is your very first relationship! Your first relationship was with your primary caregiver – this is a relationship you were born into. The dynamic or system created between the two of you is made up of pairing or emotional bonds. With each interaction that occurred between the two of you, the emotional bonds were strengthened.

As a baby you began to recognise different faces, types of touch, voices and unique smells, and associate these experiences as specific cues for comfort and safety. In fact after numerous repetitions of interactions, you were able to identify and connect to one specific face, voice, series of touches and unique smell as your primary caregiver. Other people may have also played a part in your life and may take care of you at different times. However, if these other people were not interacting with you as much as your primary caregiver you will not have developed those particular emotional bonds.

By the time you were about eight months old you internalised in your brain all the repeated interactions or bonds that had been created with the people in your life. Your brain recorded everything about them, right down to the most minuscule detail. This internalisation created and shaped an instructional blueprint in your brain and body, a template of all the people you know.

"Our mind is shaped by our relationships."
– Jacqui Christie

Your brain development

The greatest growth-spurts in your brain occur during the last trimester of pregnancy and continue into the next two years. It is widely accepted in the field of developmental psychology and neuroscience – e.g. by John Bowlby, Mary Ainsworth, Alan Sroufe, Phillip Shaver, Chris Fraley, Allan Schore – that the first 18 months of your life are the most crucial in the development of your social and emotional brain. Your social and emotional brain is part of the right hemisphere of your brain and is the first part of the brain to develop. It is the fast, nonverbal part of your brain. It's not until the second year that the left hemisphere even begins its maturation.

Traditionally, science has told us that everything in the brain prior to birth is genetic and everything that occurs after birth is learned, which is the nature versus nurture argument.

However, more recently neuropsychologists like Dr Allan Schore have found that, although you are born with genetic material in your cerebral cortex, by the time you are around ten months old this material has increased dramatically. Those neural connections continued to grow, expand and program well into the first year of life. It did not just stop at birth! Amazing! This means it is no longer just a question of nature versus nurture.

You're probably wondering how genes can become programmed after you are born? Well, it is in fact through the emotional bonds you create, through the feedback loop or attachment relationship between yourself and your primary caregiver, who becomes your primary attachment figure.

The idea of a primary attachment figure comes from the theory of attachment. This is an evolutionary, ethological and psychological theory that originated from the work of John Bowlby and was further developed by Mary Ainsworth through an observational study called 'the strange situation', a now celebrated study developed to examine a child's attachment style. Researchers put the child and her mother alone in a room containing toys and other interesting objects. The mother allowed the child to explore the room for a little time until a stranger entered the room and talked with the mother. Then the mother left the room while the stranger turned their attention and attempted to engage the child.

After several minutes, the mother returned and comforted her child and a short while later left again. This time the stranger left as well leaving the child completely alone. A few minutes later, the stranger returned and talked or played with the child. Finally, the mother returned and reunited with her child.

Ainsworth discovered that there were individual differences in how the children responded when they were separated from their mothers and when they were reunited with them. More importantly these differences could be grouped into three major styles of attachment.

"How do you learn to believe in yourself? Thru the eyes of someone else who believes in you."

– Jacqui Christie

How you 'attach' to another human being is an evolutionary process intended to keep you safe, protected and comforted. As a baby you are already primed to elicit as much care, protection and security as possible from your primary attachment figure and will continue to reach out in a variety of different ways until your needs are met. This is what we know as the survival instinct. However if your needs are not met, your brain will stop making those connections and stop

growing. The development of the brain is very specific, and requires emotionally enriched environments or experiences to reach its full potential. The right hemisphere, the social and emotional part of the brain, will only grow and mature through consistent physical and emotional care and attention with another hopefully older person, typically your primary attachment figure.

Brain pruning

At birth you have more brain cells than you need. According to Alan Schore, within the first two years of life your brain is closing down connections that are rarely used and strengthening the connections that have been reinforced. Cell death or brain pruning is a process that is more important than once believed. The experiences you share with your primary attachment figure are actually sculpting the very matter of your brain, so it really is a matter of 'neurons that fire together wire together but those that don't, die together'.

Infant attachment development

The optimum environment to create a safe and secure baby is one that is consistently emotionally rich, responsive, up close and personal, and one where the primary attachment figure and baby are highly attuned, and in sync with each other. This is achieved by bodily contact, caring touch, sounds, looks and emotions from the parent towards the baby. This type of environment allows the infant to trust that they are being emotionally supported by their primary attachment figure so they can move out and explore their world without fear and feeling safe. This is also what we call Secure Attachment.

Researchers have defined three areas of attachment that form between the child and the primary attachment figure:

1. Physical – my caregiver is nearby
2. Emotional – my caregiver understands my feelings, and
3. Cognitive – my caregiver is aware of me.

What if you were unable to receive the optimum amount of care and attention that you required? Perhaps your primary caregiver was depressed, angry or sick or otherwise emotionally unavailable for whatever reason. If this was the case the trust and bond becomes injured. From a psychobiological perspective, this breach of trust would have been like a life or death situation to you.

Even so, you would have attempted to reach out to receive as much care and attention as possible and would have developed an indirect approach to meeting your needs. This indirect approach becomes your established template and is called an Insecure Attachment. Essentially infants will modify and adapt their nurture-seeking capability to cope with the individual abilities of their primary attachment figures. For

example, if as a child your primary attachment figures were unresponsive and or insensitive to your needs you will adapt to their behaviour by taking care of yourself.

Both secure and insecure attachment styles are widespread in our population. Children will modify the way they find the nurturing they need, to cope with the abilities of their primary attachment figures.

Whichever system was created between you and your primary attachment figure becomes your most dominant and long lasting internal model of relationships. What's more it is this very system that determines your unique relational style or attachment style.

"There are ONLY relationships in this world."
– Jacqui Christie

Attachment and your relationship

The connections your brain made when you were a baby are influencing the relationships you have now. The expectations and belief systems that developed during these early years tend to persist throughout life. Just as you reached out as a baby to attract the attention of your primary attachment figure, so in adult relationships you continue to reach out for the support of your partner. If you learnt to limit your responses or needs when you were a child you will do the same with your partner. You will continue this behaviour so you can develop a sense of safety and security for yourself but also within the relationship. Imagine your attachment system is a bit like your relational safety and security system based on how safe and secure you felt in your primary relationship.

If you do not receive the contact you need from your partner, you are biologically programmed to continue attempts to obtain that security until that need is met.

This can be in a variety of different ways. Just as when you were an infant, that early template has set the scene for how you will relate to every other human being past, present and future.

"Your early template guides your current relationship."

– Jacqui Christie

The way you attach to your partner is arguably the most important predictor for how your relationship will develop. Your confidence or lack of confidence in the availability of your primary attachment figure was developed during childhood and became stored in your individual relational

template. Your individual template guides your perception of your partner's behaviours, and you will often recreate those patterns of attachment in your current relationship.

Because you both relate to each other using early templates, you and your partner become each other's surrogate primary attachment figures. In effect, you each take the place of your primary caregiver in your relationship. Even if you are not consciously aware of this, it was your templates that dictated who both of you chose to be in a relationship with. Understanding this part of your attachment allows you to recognise that it is perfectly normal to nurture and take care of each other – in fact it is essential.

Your style of attachment affects every detail in your relationship. Attachment styles influence how you think, feel and behave. Your styles can influence the way you communicate and argue, to how much hugging or touching you enjoy, to the way you and your partner separate and reunite from each other daily. A number of other relational behaviours like jealousy, infidelity, forgiveness, commitment and sexual behaviour are also influenced by your style of attachment.

By working with your attachment styles, you will have a stronger ability to face some of the insecurities and fears that are a part of your relational templates. You can discover ingrained habits you both have that keep you from having your needs met and being emotionally connected to each other. You'll begin to understand why you and your partner respond or react to each other the way you do. What's more, you can also uncover ways you are defending yourself from being emotionally connected and work toward forming a secure attachment.

If you and your partner can recognise past negative patterns of attachment in your current relationship you have the ability to stop their influence on your relationship.

Knowing how you have both formed your attachment styles can reveal to you how seemingly unrelated problems are connected. You are then better equipped to deal with the underlying issue directly instead of wasting your energy on the day to day problems of life. This in turn helps you both work through problems more effectively.

This recognition will also allow both of you to rebuild some of the communication skills necessary to produce an atmosphere of safe listening. Nonverbal communication is another part of your relationship. The way you listen, look, move, and react tells your partner whether you care, if you're being truthful and how well you're listening. Understanding your attachment style can help you become more sensitive to your partner's body language and nonverbal cues as well as your own.

As you begin to unravel what's happening between you and your partner and understand your unique couple attachment style. You can then work toward forming a secure base relationship which can be a lasting source of love, intimate connection and companionship.

There are three main attachment styles each with their own unique ways of relating. It makes sense then to not only recognise but understand what type of individual style you and your partner have.

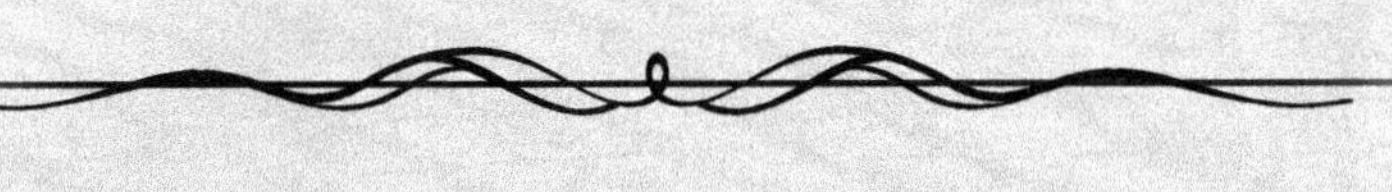

PART TWO

Your Personal Attachment Style

PART TWO

Your Personal Attachment Style

> *"Nothing is as it seems and certainly not what you think."*
>
> – Alice in Wonderland

Attachment Style Quiz

Before you can begin to understand how you and your partner relate to each other on an emotional level it's important to discover what your attachment style is. You will then find out why you think, feel and behave the way you do.

This brief quiz will measure the way you emotionally relate to your partner as well as to others in your life.

Read each of the questions, and if it applies to you, tick the circle in the columns to the right. If the question doesn't resonate with you, leave the answer blank and move to the next question.

Be truthful with yourself, using the first response that comes into your head. Try not to over think it, or answer 'correctly', as there are no right or wrong answers.

Tick only the circle next to each statement that is true for you. If the statement is not true for you then LEAVE BLANK.

	TRUE		
	A	B	C
I'm afraid that I will lose my partner's love.		○	
I tell my partner just about everything.	○		
I prefer not to be too close to my partner.			○
I often worry that my partner will not want to stay with me.		○	
I often wish that my partner's feelings for me were as strong as my feelings for him or her.		○	
I talk things over with my partner.	○		
When my partner is out of sight, I worry that he or she might become interested in someone else.		○	
I find it easy to move on after an argument.			○
I do not often worry about being abandoned.	○		
I find that my partner does not want to get as close as I would like.		○	
I get uncomfortable when my partner wants to be very close.			○
Sometimes my partner changes their feelings about me for no apparent reason.		○	
It's not difficult for me to get close to my partner.	○		
I often worry that my partner doesn't really love me.		○	
My desire to be very close sometimes scares my partner away.	○		
My partner only seems to notice me when I'm angry.		○	
I prefer not to show my partner how I feel deep down.			○
I feel comfortable sharing my private thoughts and feelings with my partner.	○		

	TRUE		
	A	B	C
I find it difficult to allow myself to depend on my partner.			○
I worry a lot about my relationship.		○	
It's easy for me to be affectionate with my partner.	○		
I don't feel comfortable opening up to my partner.			○
I rarely worry about my partner leaving me.	○		
I worry that my partner won't care about me as much as I care about them.		○	
I find it difficult to emotionally support my partner.			○
My partner is always placing demands on me.			○
I usually discuss my problems and concerns with my partner.	○		
It helps to turn to my partner in times of need.	○		
When my partner talks to me I become distracted and my energy fades.			○
Sometimes I feel angry or frustrated at my partner and I don't know why.			○
If my partner and I disagree I feel comfortable expressing my opinion.	○		
I become nervous when my partner gets too close to me.			○
I feel comfortable depending on my partner.	○		
I find it easy to put things out of my mind.			○
It makes me mad that I don't get the affection and support I need from my partner.		○	
My partner really understands me and my needs.	○		
I prefer not to share my innermost feelings with my partner.			○
I'm afraid that once my partner gets to know me, he or she won't like who I really am.		○	

*The above is based on the *Experiences in Close Relationships – Revised (ECR-R)* questionnaire developed in 2000 by Chris Fraley, Niels Waller and Kelly Brennan. For the fully validated attachment questionnaire please go to Dr Chris Fraley's website at: www.web-research-design.net/cgi-bin/crq/crq.pl

How to score

Number of ticked circles in column A: ______________________

Number of ticked circles in column B: ______________________

Number of ticked circles in column C: ______________________

There are three main attachment styles, each a product of the style of attachment you developed with your primary caregiver. The more ticks you have in each column the more likely this is your attachment style.

Most ticks in column A = Secure attachment style

Most ticks in column B = Ambivalent attachment style

Most ticks in column C = Avoidant attachment style.

It would be great idea if your partner were to complete the quiz as well. This will allow you to begin a conversation about each of your styles and how they are affecting your relationship. Of course this may not always be possible and given that it is you reading the book let's concentrate on you.

Each of the attachment styles is discussed in the next chapter. Have a read and see if you find yourself (or your partner) inside one of these chapters.

The Three Styles

The three styles of attachment do not stand alone. In fact they are all only points along a continuum, so you may find yourself sitting anywhere along the line.

Avoidant (insecure)	Secure	Ambivalent (insecure)
· distancing	· relationship first	· clinging
· self-regulating	· flexible	· need others to regulate them
· fear of being engulfed	· emotionally solid	· fear of abandonment
· emotional suppressor	· quick repairers	· angry resistant
· keeps secret	· clear communicators	· therapist in the room

*Adapted from Tatkin (2003-2014)

The middle style is securely attached and the other two are insecure attachment styles. You may relate to being right in the middle or you may be anywhere along the continuum of attachment. Perhaps in some situations you are further up one end and in others you are at a different point. This may happen occasionally but in general you will always default to one particular style and even more so in times of stress or conflict.

Attachment styles are stable but depend on the person you are in a relationship with. For example, with your friendships or work colleagues you may find you relate in a more secure way, however with your partner you behave in an avoidant or ambivalent style. The more intimate you are in a relationship

the more you will experience the characteristics of that style. The characteristics of each style were developed from your earliest memories, which are deeply embedded in your social and emotional brain, so they are pretty much hard-wired.

Don't panic if you have identified yourself as having either of the two insecure styles, as approximately forty percent of the population falls into either avoidant or ambivalent styles (Moullin, Waldfogel and Washbrook 2014). Remember all these styles are perfectly normal.

Secure Attachment

I trust that you are always there for me.

It is easy and natural for you to be in a relationship. You enjoy being truly intimate with your partner and don't become overly worried about your relationship. You have developed this style of attachment because as a child you viewed your primary attachment figure as a secure base from which to venture out into the world. Your primary attachment figure was close to you regularly, talking, using lots of physical contact and making you feel safe emotionally. As well as effectively managing their own stress, your primary caregiver responded to your cues and signals and soothed you when you needed it. More importantly though they would have repaired any disconnect between you as soon as possible. This unique interaction was like a well-tuned dance between the two of you. This assurance allowed you to come and go with a sense of safety, secure in the knowledge that your caregiver was consistently there for you and that you could depend on them no matter what. This is what developmental psychologist's call secure-autonomous. Being secure allows you to be truly autonomous and comes from an inner certainty that things will work out for you.

As an adult with a secure attachment, you operate in a very similar fashion. Because your template of attachment is secure you are able to draw on your partner as a source of emotional comfort and internal regulation, and provide the same for them. You are attuned to your partner's needs and are able to read their cues and signals and respond appropriately and in a timely fashion. When arguments occur, you are able to repair the rift or misunderstanding sooner rather than later. You are there for your partner, can offer emotional support when needed and feel comfortable sharing your problems and successes with them.

Being alone or being with others does not cause you undue concern. You have the ability to move between the two states of being alone to being with other people with great ease and feel neither overwhelmed nor abandoned. You are not afraid of physical closeness so when your partner wants to be close you don't respond with anger, compliance, withdrawal

or dismissal. Instead, you embrace the opportunity and feel comfortable to reach out for emotional or physical intimacy. Because you are collaborative and cooperative you will expect the same in return from your partner. One of the most important differences between your style and that of the insecure styles is that you value your relationship above most if not all other things in your life.

Research has shown that securely attached people are more satisfied at work and experience more career and job security. Having a secure attachment gives you more energy and internal resources to function at a higher level emotionally, socially, and academically. Being comfortable and secure in your relationships gives you a significant psychological boost in your work ethic and courage to move out into the world. This allows you to feel more positive and enjoy a more successful life.

If it's good for you then it's good for me too.

Avoidant Attachment

The master of the mask.

It's easy for you to spend time in your own company. In fact you enjoy spending time on your own and find it less stressful than interacting with your partner. You prefer to keep your partner at a distance and tend to see yourself as low maintenance.

This attachment style has been developed because it was uncomfortable for your primary caregiver to have you too physically close to them or to interact with you for any substantial amount of time. Instead they encouraged you to entertain and play by yourself. This made it difficult for you to depend on your caregiver for safety and security as they were often physically and emotionally unavailable to you. When they were available they were dismissive and disparaging toward you or even neglectful. You learned to depend on yourself rather than others.

An adult with an avoidant attachment style behaves in a similar fashion. Even though you may want to be close to others, attempts by your partner to be emotionally close make you feel uncomfortable, so you look for ways to avoid this closeness. You deny your need for relationship dependence and will feel embarrassed at the thought of even having such needs and will underestimate others care and support of you .

It is hard for you discuss anything emotional, instead you prefer to put things behind you and move on putting more of your attention and focus on the future. You dismiss your partners concerns or worries and don't express your own. It is extremely important to you to maintain your independence and self-reliance, so you may not even be aware that you have emotional needs and will deny as much if asked directly.

In an experiment, researchers asked avoidant adults to discuss losing their partner. By using skin conductance measures they found that they were just as physiologically distressed as other attachment styles, however, they were better at suppressing their thoughts and feelings. You learnt to do this as an adaptive measure from your early experiences as a child. It is a defence mechanism, a way of coping with the discomfort of the emotion that may creep up inside of you. However, to your partner you may appear disconnected, or worse, not even interested.

Research has found that individuals with an avoidant attachment experience more fear of failure, avoid discovering new ways to achieve in their life and are more prone to resist challenging yet potentially rewarding activities. In the work setting they exhibit more conflict with co-workers, lower levels of job satisfaction and can experience more difficulties with relationships outside of work. Because they often view others as unavailable, unresponsive or punishing, they will distance themselves from other staff to avoid emotional closeness.

Avoidant individuals have a negative view of others, leading to obsessive self-reliance, independence, and difficulties in trust and dependence on others.

People who have an avoidant attachment style tend to operate in the world through what I call zones. You learnt from a young age to internally manage or regulate your emotions and do this so automatically that is out of your conscious awareness. You tend to become deeply engrossed in what you are doing and are so far in your zone that when your partner approaches you it feels like you're being dragged out to talk to them. Being forced to shift from being alone with whatever you are doing to interacting with your partner can feel like a physical shock as you are jolted from your dreamlike state. Your partner moving toward you may seem like an invasion of your privacy or your time alone, both things you value greatly.

Jenny and John

It's the weekend and Jenny and John are both at home. Jenny is in the study with the door closed. She's been feeling a lot of pressure lately from her boss to get the project in on time and is deeply engrossed in her work. John has been busy working on the house and has noticed she is not around. He gently opens the study door and says, "You're very quiet in here. What are you up to?" Jenny continues working with no response. John asks again, "Just checking if you would like a cuppa?" Jenny continues working with no response. John then firmly says "Jenny I am talking to you. Can you answer me please!?" Jenny is now looking at John with an annoyed expression on her face and says "Huh! Can't you see what I'm doing! I'm busy! What is it!?"

Jenny has an avoidant attachment style and is in her zone. She is emotionally regulating herself and managing the emotional pressure she feels from her boss by focussing her attention on her work. She is so focussed that she remains unaware of John until he changes his tone of voice towards her. Because John is then in close proximity to her and his tone of voice is tense she lashes out at him. Jenny's response is very similar to a baby startled by a loud noise. As well as the shock of noticing John, Jenny also has difficulty emotionally moving from being in the zone of focussing on work to being in the zone of interacting with John.

This will resonate if you have an avoidant style. It can feel a bit jarring sometimes moving from being alone to interacting with other people. It's not often a smooth transition for you as during your early development you were not exposed to too much one on one time or interaction with your caregivers. Because you are not used to continually being in direct contact with people, it makes you feel uncomfortable. You are behaving as you naturally would, as you always have. How your attachment style has been wired in your brain.

If Jenny had decided to come out of the office and look for John, we would have seen a very different scenario. Because she made the choice to come out of her zone it is not emotionally threatening to her she is ready, available, to spend some time with John.

Don't get too close unless I ask you.

Ambivalent Attachment

I love you and hate you all at the same time.

You desperately want to be with your partner but at the same time can't trust that they really want to be in the relationship with you. You have a tendency to pull your partner toward you but then physically or verbally push them away.

Like the other two styles of attachment your style goes back to your primary attachment figures way of interacting with you, which, in the ambivalent case was preoccupied and inconsistent. They had an on-again off-again approach to parenting. Sometimes attuning and tending to your needs but sometimes not. Your primary attachment figure was sometimes insensitive and intrusive or even anxious and hostile but at other times appropriate and nurturing. You were on an emotional swing of needs being met and not met and could not work out what the magic was that caused your caregiver to respond to you. Because of this inconsistency, you were on the constant lookout for clues on how to influence your caregiver's responses.

It is likely that from a young age you had to take emotional and or physical care of one of your primary caregivers. This was because they tended to feel overwhelmed, easily frustrated and had difficulty coping with being a parent at times. This behaviour led you to sometimes feel needed and wanted but sometimes rejected. Consequently, you didn't feel secure and if distressed were difficult to soothe.

Similarly as an adult, you experience the push and pull of emotions within you. You dream of your partner pursuing you and are always waiting for this to happen. You seek constant reassurance but can lash out when your needs aren't fully met. You tend to overly focus on your partner and worry about

your relationship. It's important to you to feel wanted in your relationship but sometimes you feel that you are needy, too much and a burden to your partner. This same belief can keep you stuck in the past, replaying past hurts and injustices and not being able to focus or move forward in your relationship. Deep down you expect to be rejected or abandoned by your partner and this can also flow onto relationships with other friends and colleagues.

Because you experienced some emotional and physical closeness during your early development, you are comfortable talking about emotions and are verbally expressive. But because that closeness was inconsistent, when you reach out to your partner you have great difficulty receiving what you want. You will often pull back from them, sabotage or push them away either physically or emotionally. This behaviour can at times be aggressive. If you have been away from your partner, when you meet up again you may feel annoyed frustrated or even angry and not understand why.

Research has found that, similar to people with avoidant styles, people with an ambivalent attachment style also experience more fear of failure, avoid exploring new and or different ways to achieve and are more prone to resist challenging yet potentially rewarding activities. Ambivalently attached people in particular feel unappreciated and misunderstood in the workplace and expect to be undervalued by co-workers.

They are anxious about their relationships at work and job performance and this insecurity and fear of rejection makes it difficult to feel emotionally committed and provide unconditional assistance in the workplace.

Adam and Anna

Adam and Anna are engaged and have lived together for three years. Anna has gone out with her friends for the evening and Adam has decided to stay at home. Anna tells Adam that she will be home by midnight and will call or text him on her way home. Before she leaves she gives Adam a kiss and a hug but his body becomes rigid and he turns his head away. She tells him she loves him and she will miss him. Adam complains she is always going out and leaving him on his own, and her friends are obviously more important than he is. He asks Anna to call as soon as she gets to the restaurant.

A couple of hours go by and Adam has become extremely anxious. He worries about what Anna might be up to and has started texting her with questions such as "How are things going?", "How long are you going to be?" and "When are you coming home?". He receives texts back from Anna saying "I'm having a good time", "I'll be a few hours yet" and "I'll call you on the way home". She also lets him know the restaurant is very busy and she can't hear herself think. As the evening progresses Adam gives up on texting and starts calling Anna repeatedly. When she doesn't answer he angrily leaves messages on her phone, firstly demanding to know why she hasn't picked up and later to remind her of just how inconsiderate she is.

Adam and Anna (continued)

It's about 1 am when Anna gets home. Adam is waiting at the door and as soon as she gets in he begins to shout at her. He tells her how inconsiderate she is and how she only ever thinks of herself. Anna tries to tell him that she went to call him earlier but couldn't get a phone signal. As Adam's anger and frustration increases he tells her that he has been up all night imagining the worst and starts to snap questions at her in an accusing tone, "Who were you with?", "Why didn't you call when you said you would" and "I can't believe you would do that to me!" Anna tries a couple of times to respond to Adam but he continues berating her, saying "I'm just not sure of you at all!" and "If you ever do this to me again I'm done!" He ends by announcing he'll be sleeping on the couch tonight. Anna is still standing in the lounge as the lights go off and he lies down on the couch.

This scenario will resonate with you if you have an ambivalent attachment style. Being away from your partner can cause you a lot of anxiety and emotional pain. It can be difficult for you to shift from being with your partner to being alone. You may remember some of your early experiences with your primary caregiver with lots of one on one time. You also remember though, the times when your caregiver was frustrated with you or unavailable. Remembering this causes you to feel resentment and anger. This is a part of you behaving as you naturally would, as you always have. This is how your attachment style has been wired in your brain.

If Adam had explained to Anna more fully how anxious he feels when he is left alone we may have seen a different outcome. Sharing his underlying feelings with Anna would have allowed him to calm down as he would have felt heard and understood.

Why do I always have to wait for you?

How does your style affect your relationship?

Now you know what style you are, and perhaps what style your partner is, you can view your relationship in a new light and begin to see the dynamics you both bring in to it.

You can start to understand why you both behave the way you do. Knowing which style you both have opens the door to understanding how those styles work together, and where they tend to butt up against each other. Sometimes labelling is helpful. It can give you a reason for behaviours, rather than blaming the person for intentionally acting in a certain way. This will help you head off arguments before they escalate, and find ways to communicate more effectively.

First of all, spend some time looking at how your attachment style works with your partner's style to create the relationship dynamics you are dealing with. Are you both the same style or are you bringing different approaches into the relationship?

Insecure relationships

There are three different combinations of insecure attachments depending on the personal styles of you and your partner: ambivalent with ambivalent, avoidant with avoidant or one of the most common relationship combinations, avoidant with ambivalent. Whatever the combination, insecure couples are characterised by inflexibility, with rigidity of thought and experiences, and will often behave like two married single people. This is where the couple live separate lives or take up separate activities or positions on topics with little awareness of their own or their partner's thoughts, emotions or experiences. They spend very little time truly getting to know each other or being in each other's space.

Because of their early insecure attachments, there is an unconscious focus on what is or isn't safe in the relationship, which gets acted out many times throughout their life together. The insecure couple tend to play emotional games with each other, such as communicating indirectly often with a negative intention. Tricking or testing their partner to see if they really care for them, not talking for days when hurts or injuries have occurred, or deliberately doing something to hurt their partner in retaliation. The insecure couple find it very hard to work together when faced with difficult times, as they have very little or nothing to protect them against

each other and the vulnerabilities that can occur throughout a lifetime.

Two of the major issues the insecure couple have to grapple with are trust and fear of each other and other people, due to their early deprived experiences of safety and security. This does not mean that as a couple they do not want to experience the freedom of safety and security, they most definitely do, it is just very difficult for either of them to trust that that will ever happen in their relationship. Even though research has found that insecure relationships tend to be unfair, unjust and insensitive they are still remarkably stable and predictable.

Tim and Tania

Tim and Tania were away for the weekend at one of their favourite destinations, and eating at a new restaurant. Tania became agitated as the meal is took a while to come to the table. She noticed that newer patrons were being brought their meals and pointed this out to Tim saying it's not fair and not right. Tim was uncomfortable with what Tania was saying and in a low hissing tone reminded her that their meal will take some time as they had ordered a speciality. He comments on her facial expression, pointing out how angry she looks and that there must be something wrong with her. Thirty minutes have gone by since the couple arrived at the restaurant and Tania has been complaining constantly. When Tim asks her what's going on, she stares stone-faced ahead of her. Tim again asks why she is taking it out on him, suggesting that she should just let it go.

Tim and Tania (continued)

Tania is now staring furiously at Tim and hisses that he never takes her side on anything and it is ridiculous that they should have to wait 45 minutes for a steamed fish. Tim suggests they wait five more minutes, then ask for their money back and leave. He also continues to stare blankly out of the window.

The waiter arrives at their table apologising profusely for the wait and advising them that their meal will be five more minutes. Tania instantly relaxes her body, smiles and begins to talk to Tim about his new silver wrist band they had bought together at the craft market. Tim looks away from her. A few minutes go by and sure enough their meal arrives. When the fish is put down in front of them Tim gives out a sigh of disgust. Looking at the fish in dismay he points out how small it is and how they were promised it would be enough for two. He complains that he is paying all this money for vegetables and rice. Tim becomes more and more agitated complaining how disgusting it all is and how he is going to have a burger after the meal. Tania listens quietly while eating the fish and vegetables and says how nice the food is.

A few moments later the couple leave the restaurant, Tania is feeling contented after eating and is happily chatting away and not noticing Tim's demeanour. Tim however has become outwardly angry at Tania and begins to blame her for spoiling the evening, saying that she could have let it go.

Tim and Tania (continued)

He continues on about the food, the price and how the evening has been ruined. He suggests they go next door to a burger joint because he is starving so orders a fish burger. As he throws the food down his throat he complains how the burger has no flavour. The couple walk to the car in silence. They hear music coming from a nearby hotel and can see the band through the window. Tania pauses to watch and comments how good the band sounds and how much fun it looks. She mentions that they could have gone there and Tim adds, yes if you had wanted to wait in the queue. On the drive back Tania continues chatting, reminding Tim that the food was really quite nice and that it was a great pity that his burger was not as he'd hoped. They arrive back at the hotel, and Tania continues being chatty, asking Tim if he would like something to drink or something sweet to eat.

But by now Tim is furious. He lashes out at Tania and berates her for her behaviour. Again he says that there must be something seriously wrong with her and wonders how she could act as if nothing has happened after she ruined their evening together. He also points out how he had asked her multiple times to calm down and she wouldn't then her demeanour completely changed as soon as the food came out. As Tim is yelling at her, Tania sits quietly with her head down. After a while Tim pauses, which is Tania's cue to begin yelling and remind him that as usual he did not support her when they were in the restaurant.

Tim and Tania (continued)

If he had just agreed with her in the first place none of this would have happened. But no, he could never do that, he was nice to the waiter and acted as if nothing has happened rather than support her. She shouts, "Oh what's the point. I'm going to bed!" and storms off to the bathroom slamming the door behind her. Tim says, "Suits me fine". By the time Tania comes out of the bathroom the lights are off in the room and Tim is in bed. The couple go to sleep in silence. After a few minutes, Tim is snoring and Tania cries softly until she falls asleep.

Exercise:

Did you guess what attachment styles Tim and Tania are? Tim is avoidant and Tania ambivalent. Their relational styles are not extreme because they have spent a number of years learning how to communicate with each other with more safety and security. However there are still key areas where they come unstuck. And this was one of them.

See if you can also:

- Notice key areas where they had difficulty.
- Spot some of their insecure behaviours.
- Write down how they could have supported each other differently.
- Think about how you would react to your partner if you were Tim or Tania.

"Create a relationship built on love and trust."

– Jacqui Christie

Secure relationships

A secure couple will put their relationship first, making the relationship a priority against all other relationships and protecting the relationship at all costs. Stan Tatkin talks of four main principles that guide a secure relationship:

1. True mutuality
2. Fairness
3. Justice, and
4. Sensitivity.

Tatkin believes that, in a secure relationship, the emphasis is on both partners working toward the good of each other as quickly as possible.

The couple work toward a win–win outcome for each other in all that they do. They both expect the other to be responsive and available, are not overly anxious or threatened by getting too close or too far away from each other, and don't perceive conflict as a threat to the relationship. The couple have a strong commitment to one another and a positive view of themselves, others, and their relationship.

Research has found securely attached individuals are able to communicate openly during conflicts, and are also able to apply a variety of strategies to negotiate win-win outcomes with their partner.

The secure couple both offer and expect cooperation and a mutual focus on keeping the relationship running smoothly.

The couple support each other emotionally when required, for example one partner will be soothing when the other partner feels distressed and vice versa. This repairing of hurts or relieving of emotional injuries is offered as quickly as possible. Tatkin tells us that in this relationship the couple protect each other at all times, especially when with other people. The secure couple incorporate playfulness into their relationship and both reap the rewards from the novelty and fun that comes from this. They feel secure and connected to each other, while allowing each other to move freely, because they know they are safe in each other's care.

Emotional game playing is not a part of this relationship and communication is clear and creative. When they were children, these two were safe and secure, so their social and emotional brains have been sufficiently developed. This enables them to read faces, emotions and tone of voice really well. Securely attached couples also experience longer lasting relationships, due to their ability to focus on maintaining secure bonds with each other above all else.

Paula and Peter

Paula and Peter are going to Peter's Christmas work function. They are both getting dressed and discussing how they think the evening will go.

Paula is gently laughing as she moves up close to Peter and says, "Can you remember last year when your boss kept talking to me for hours and I couldn't get away?". Peter looks into her eyes and nods his head in agreement. Paula continues, "and you didn't do much better. His wife had you enthralled with stories of her vegetable garden". They both laugh at the memories. Peter then says, "Okay let's talk about how we are we going to manage it tonight then?" "Great yes," says Paula as she fixes his tie. "Ummm, how about we use our secret signal to let each other know if we need rescuing? Remember how well it worked for us at the Berringer's party a couple of weeks ago?". Peter smiles as he pulls Paula closer towards him and whispers into her ear, "Yes it certainly did work didn't it... I'm not sure Ms Priest was too happy though". The couple roar with laughter knowing how well they both did that night at managing outside threats to their relationship. Paula smiles and says, "Ok then I will take my tissue out of my bag and blow my nose if I start to get cornered and you will..." Peter jumps in and says, "I will start coughing Let's make sure we come back and touch base with each other occasionally through the night too". Paula nods in agreement and says, "Yes that will give us less chance of being cornered. Now let's get a move on or there won't be a party to go to".

Can you choose the style of relationship you have?

Unfortunately, not all of us have the kind of secure relationship enjoyed by Paula and Peter. The good news is that even if you and your partner have insecure attachment styles you can acquire powerful skills to rewire your relationship and turn things around. Yes, it is possible to relate to each other as if you had the kind of secure relationship you have dreamt of. When you create your own it's called a *secure base relationship.*

A secure base relationship allows you to both behave toward each other as if you had a childhood filled with secure attachment. Even if you and your partner both have insecure attachment styles, through understanding each other's styles and having the commitment of working towards having a safe and secure relationship you can create one. Just like you created the relationship you have now.

You can only create a secure base relationship together as a couple. It's not something you can really do effectively alone. It's true you may reap some benefits from understanding yourself but you both need to be working on this as a team to create major change in your relationship. Imagine you're sitting on a mountaintop feeling completely Zen and at one with the universe. You've done so much personal development in your life and you truly feel and believe that you have a deep understanding of yourself and why you behave the way you

do. You come down from the mountaintop and there is your partner waiting for you. What happens? Are you still Zen? Are you still at one with the universe? Generally, the answer to this question is no. Before you know it, there are misattunements between you and your partner and perhaps even an argument. Why does this happen? Because you are no longer alone, you are interacting with your partner who by biological design brings up all of your unmet needs and desires and most likely has a different style of relating than you.

Recent research has found that if you are not able to successfully use your partner as a secure base and a source of comfort, over time this wears down your level of intimacy with one another. You are unaware of how your behaviour impacts your partner which leads to less commitment to working on your relationship. This results in less ability to resolve your disagreements in healthy, constructive ways. If you feel distant with each other you are less likely to want to repair, maintain or improve your relationship.

So it makes good sense to use your partner as your secure base, I mean who else is there to use instead?

Working together though, you and your partner can move toward the middle of the relationship continuum and create the secure relationship you want.

You've already started by learning what style you are, and so can start to understand why you both behave the way you do. Because your individual attachment style is pretty much hard-wired understanding your styles gives you both a reason for your behaviours, rather than blaming the person for intentionally acting in a certain way. This will help you head off arguments before they escalate, and also find ways to communicate more effectively.

If your aim is to create a relationship that is connected, warm and lasting – this doesn't just happen through wishful thinking. After a lifetime of practising the way you have been currently relating to each other it can be hard to change the way you think and respond.

It takes a commitment from both of you to seeing things differently and being willing to try new things and do things differently.

"There is only a WE because the whole is greater than the sum of its parts."

– Jacqui Christie

PART THREE

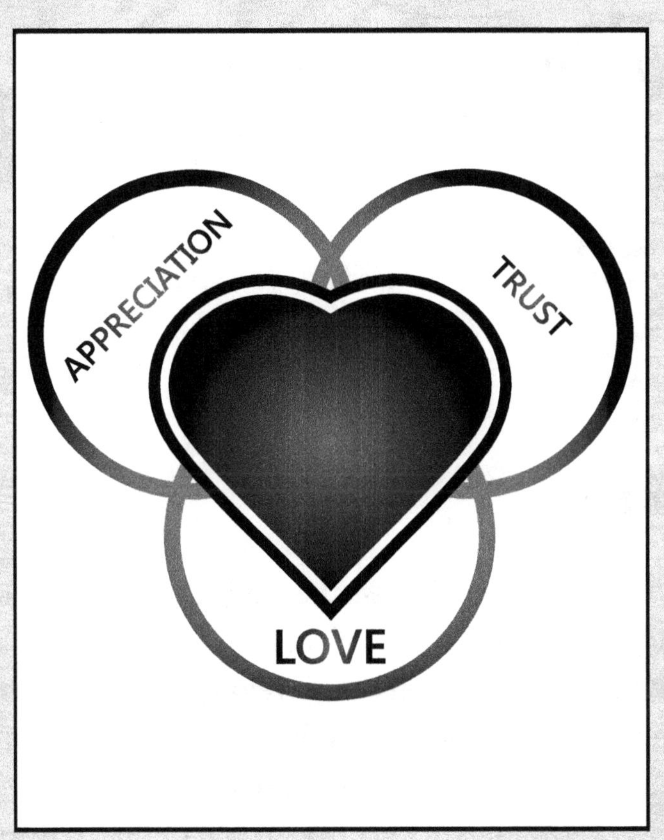

Principles to Rewire Your Relationship

PART THREE

Principles to Rewire your Relationship

"Be a safe harbour for your partner."

– Jacqui Christie

How to begin

Sit down together and discuss the kinds of principles you want to incorporate into your relationship. You can use the ones provided in this book, you can develop your own ones or you can use a combination of both. Principles are like guidelines that you make with each other about how your relationship will work or what it will look like. You don't need to agree on every single thing together but you do need to discuss fully what kinds of principles you both want to follow. Then you both need to write them down. Be realistic so only write down the principles that you can both actually keep.

The seven guiding principles for a secure base

1. Your relationship is a separate identity

Your relationship is a separate identity from each of you individually and needs to be fed, watered and nourished. There are three entities operating in the relationship, with the relationship being the priority. This means your relationship has to be placed above your work, above the children, above your aging parents, above your business and above your hobbies and friends. You and your partner both need to be the number one in each other's lives. Imagine you have a garden; if you don't look after the garden the grass and weeds will grow and in time your garden will become completely overgrown. But if the garden is tended and taken care of with the weeds pulled up, plants pruned, grass clipped, seeds planted and pathways swept and tidied, then your garden will remain lush with room to grow more life. Just like taking care of a garden, the secure couple look after their relationship and continually tend to it.

2. Mutual commitment

Mutual commitment involves the two of you as partners being committed to each other even in times of stress. Work on your relationship together for the benefit of both of you. When you have both agreed to truly commit to each other it is easier for you both to face the difficulties and the challenges that come with life. Mutual commitment means to be wholly and solely in the relationship, without giving yourself an emotional back door to get out of the relationship. It means understanding that you and your partner will support each other emotionally, financially, mentally, spiritually, verbally, all to the best of your ability, through good times and bad. Developing and incorporating mutual commitment into your relationship enables trust and respect to grow between you.

If you are married you would have made some kind of vows to each other. When was the last time you looked at them and how are you both going at implementing them? I'm sure your intention when you made your wedding vows for them to be pledges about how you both envisioned your relationship and how you were going to take care of each other. Just like any plan they need to be relooked at and perhaps adjusted or added to. If you have not made any formal commitments to each other perhaps now is the time to start. Ask each other Is the life we want to be living? If it isn't, make a plan for gradual change in any area that needs it.

When you agree to live by the principle of mutual commitment you need to discuss what form your commitments are going to take. The commitments need to reflect your relational life together for example, if *x* happens with each other we both agree to do *y* or *z*. After you have both decided together what

the agreements are, you both need to verbally agree to follow them. It's also a good idea if you read each agreement out to one another. The practice of reading them out loud allows you both to hear each other acknowledge how important your relationship is to each of you. There's something very powerful about hearing your partner make commitments to you just as much as it is for you to say it to your partner.

Examples of mutual commitments can be:

- We both agree that we put each other first above all others, including our children, parents and especially work.
- If one of us causes distress in the other, we agree that whoever has caused the distress has to make it right straight away for the both of us.
- If we go to one of your work functions, we agree that during the function you will come and find me and touch base to see how I am.

This is YOUR relationship. You both have the power to create the mutual relational style that you want to have together. A secure base relationship.

"Two brains are better than one so why not join with your partners to maximise your relationship."

– Jacqui Christie

3. Collaboration

Just as a common prerequisite for employment is the ability to work in a team, the ability to work collaboratively, this same approach is required in your relationship. Teamwork is crucial to creating a safe and secure relationship – what's good for your partner is going to be good for you too. Remember the old adage 'two brains are better than one', so use your partner's brain as an extension of your own and allow them to use yours. In this way, you can both create or manoeuvre through difficult times to something that works for the both of you.

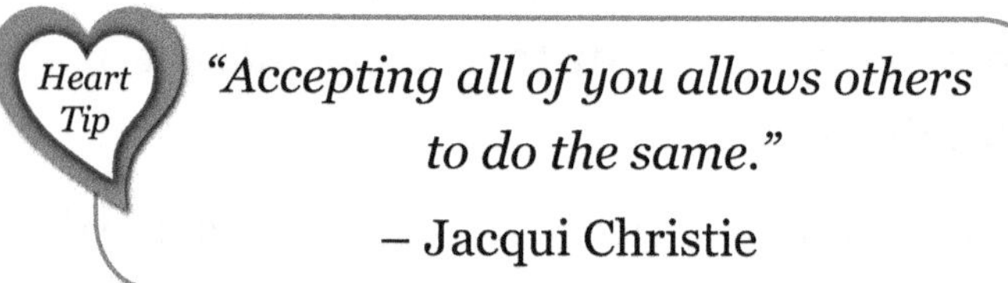

Heart
Tip
"Accepting all of you allows others to do the same."
– Jacqui Christie

4. Acceptance

By accepting your partner as they are, you can also accept yourself. The way you and your partner behave toward each other is hard-wired in your brains from childhood. Therefore your energy is wasted trying to change their behaviour to something that you think suits you more. Accepting each other's personal attachment style will allow you both the freedom to be who you are. It's still important to find ways to create harmony, but one of those is to realise what you

can and can't change. Then you both have the opportunity to become something greater than you are as individuals.

"By depending on each other we are honouring our relationship."

– Jacqui Christie

5. Interdependance

You and your partner are tied together with an invisible thread. You may not see this right now but there is one sure-fire way to check. If you are upset then it is very common for your partner to be upset too. If your partner is having a bad day then you will notice that it begins to affect you too. You and your partner depend on each other for survival and for the safety and security of your relationship. As a couple you each depend on your partner to fill your sexual, social, and emotional needs, such as friendship, communication, nurturing, appreciation, learning, love and touch. And because you love each other, it's normal to feel attached, to desire closeness, to be concerned for each another, and to depend upon each other. Remember your partner is your surrogate primary attachment figure and just as a baby depends on their primary caregiver for love, care and nurturing, you too can depend on each other. So go with the flow and give yourself permission to honour your own needs as well as your partner's.

"Be who you REALLY are warts and all."

– Jacqui Christie

6. Honest communication

Talk to each other even when it hurts. Talk to each other especially when it hurts. Talk to each other sooner rather than later. Don't sit on or push down what you want to talk about. If you're worried that your partner is not feeling loved or appreciated then ask them about it, and let your partner know you're willing to solve the problem together. Honest communication means talking to your partner about things you have never talked about to anyone before in your life. It means being completely vulnerable with your partner using an open heart. If you notice something that your partner does for you even if its small, then let them know that you have noticed. Tell how it makes you feel. If you feel loved by something they have done then it's even more important to let them know. Listen to your partner when they tell you how they feel, because most of the time they are trying to tell you something about themselves, not you. Your partner is your best shoulder to cry on.

Honest communication is also about how you portray yourself to your partner. If you believe that it will be more beneficial to your relationship to hide parts of yourself, you

are not only denying yourself but are denying your partner the opportunity to fully know you. Your partner will be communicating and relating to an illusion, a false version of you. Remember, no one is perfect and everyone has deficits. Hiding your emotions behind a wall is not going to give you the kind of relationship you desire.

If you allow your whole personality to shine through, even the bits you dislike, you are allowing your partner to do the same. When you both accept yourselves it allows you to emotionally stretch and grow in your relationship. Always be who you truly are to your partner.

The earlier you talk to your partner about your feelings to do with a certain subject the easier it will be for each of you. Trying to push things aside or let things go (where do they go?) will cause resentment and anger to build up inside you. This then tends to come out distorted, or a way that you don't want it to.

A brief example:

- Begin by checking out with each other the meaning of certain words. For example 'support', ask each other what this means to the both of you.
- Support can be emotional, verbal or financial in nature.
- It's important to know what your partner is meaning if and when they use this word.

- Explore and discuss different words or ideas with your partner.
- This helps you both to be on the same page when you are communicating.

"The greatest gift that you and your partner can give each other is all of you."

– Jacqui Christie

7. Create new memories together

It's important for both of you to create new experiences together. Your brain loves novelty; novel experiences trigger the production of dopamine, the neurotransmitter responsible for feelings of pleasure and motivation. When you are sharing a new experience that is exciting and fun tell each other how you feel in that very moment. Perhaps you are looking at a waterfall or a sunset together and you say to each other, "This is just wonderful, I'm so glad you are here with me right now and we are doing this together". In this way you both experience a mutual chemical high of watching the sunset together. You have created not only a shared memory but a shared physiological experience that you will both recall for years.

Following these principles will not only enrich your relationship, it can also enable you to feel safe and secure with each other. Feeling safe and secure is the gold standard in a relationship; there is nothing more valuable. It allows you to be who you are without fear and allows your partner to approach you, safe in the knowledge that you will accept them. These principles will help you learn to always trust each other so together you can work towards creating that secure base for each other.

"Focus on what you want in your relationship instead of what you don't want."

– Jacqui Christie

Six techniques to transform your relationship

Repair Quickly

Forgiveness, apologising, making things right and fixing things are all pointed in the same direction, which is repair. In a secure relationship repair means working toward easing the pain of your partner. To be able to do this you need to forget your pride or fear or whatever else is getting in the way of repairing, and focus on your partner and healing the rift between you. This means soothing your partner, but it also means taking action quickly.

Research has found that part of our brain is involved in emotional memory, memory consolidation, face recognition and facial expression so the time you take to repair is critical. Essentially, if you have hurt your partner, and don't make good or mend that hurt *as soon as possible*, whatever you have said or done will rapidly move into your partner's long-term memory. Think about what it's like for the two of you when you go to sleep on an argument without apologising or mending anything. The longer you keep your partner waiting the more that incident goes into long-term memory. So if you have a partner that seems to remember nearly everything hurtful or painful that you have said to them. They only continue to remember because that hurt has not been repaired quickly enough.

As a couple you both need to take responsibility to reduce the distress of each other. If you upset your partner and don't do anything about it, or worse avoid talking about what just happened, then there will be repercussions, and they will probably be for you! If your partner is distressed by something you have said or done they are probably hyper-activated so they are not really in the best position to repair at that time. So it is your responsibility to do something to reduce or alleviate the pain of your partner. Why would you do this, simply because you can. You are probably the only person and certainly the best person that can alleviate your partner's pain and distress because you are attached

to each other. Researchers have also noted the ability to repair is a major predictor for the longevity or otherwise in a relationship. Finally, you would take care of your partner in this way because you are coming from the principle of mutual commitment.

Face Time

"Look into each other's eyes and reconnect again."

– Jacqui Christie

Learn to read each other's faces. If you are talking to your partner really look at their face. When you avoid eye contact it makes it easier for your nervous system to become hyper-activated. The amygdala is the part of the brain that triggers the fight, flight or freeze response. Maintaining eye contact and with your partner while you are talking is one way to reduce this trigger. Even if you are not talking, observe your partner face, take the time to learn what each of the different expressions on their face mean. If in doubt you can always ask each other what an expression means so you can slowly become an expert on each other's faces. By becoming an expert at reading your partner's face, the micro-expressions, the eye movements and anything else you may notice makes it easier to pay attention to your partner's cues toward you and allows you both to move more in tune with each other. And if you are more in tune or attuned with each other you will find it easier to regulate each other's emotional state.

Just on this point, I know of many couples who believe the best place to talk about their most difficult topics is in the car. When your eyes are facing forward you are unable to read each other's faces accurately as you are using your peripheral vision. From a biological perspective talking while using your peripheral vision is another way of activating your amygdala and you or your partner may start to behave as if there is danger. If you want to talk about something meaningful in your relationship, then please talk face to face.

Manage your stress

Ongoing external pressure can cause internal stress in our bodies. Stress can come in many forms such as major life changes for example marriage, pregnancy or new baby, moving interstate, working too much, death of a loved one, loss of income, the list is a long one.

In today's world one continual way your stress level is increasing is through the constant interaction with technology. Having your technology or screens always on can induce stress in your body as you are regularly feeling demanded upon to look at them answer them and deal with whatever is

happening on the screen right now. It's a very subtle pressure but a real one and needs to be managed. So switch off all of your screens... Yes, all of them... Ask yourself do I really need to do this right now, this minute and if the answer is no then it can wait until tomorrow. It's much easier to do than people believe, but it's also very important especially when you come home and are with your partner. As screens are a triangle your partner is likely to feel pushed out in favour of the screen as it takes time away from the time you have with each other. (See chapter on Triangles.)

From a biological perspective when you or your partner is under stress your body secretes stress hormones, cortisol and epinephrine (adrenaline). High levels of these hormones in your system can wreak havoc on your brain in terms of functioning and structure. Chronic stress can affect your health, causing symptoms from headaches, worrying, high blood pressure, and chest pain to heart palpitations, skin rashes, and loss of sleep. If either of you is experiencing stress it is likely your relationship is suffering and causing tension between the two of you.

As with most things the focus is not so much on the stress but how you deal with the stress in your day-to-day life and particularly in your relationship. Emotional support has been found to be an important part in preventing or reducing stress. Research has found that people who enjoy close relationships with their partner's, their family and friends receive the emotional support that indirectly helps to sustain them at times of stress and crisis (check out the sixth principal).

If you work on being as attuned as possible to each other you will be able to notice small changes. Pay attention if you or your partner is having difficulty sleeping or is consistently sighing or there is a lack of motivation or unusual snappiness. Gently approach your partner about what you've noticed and start a healing conversation together. Learning practices such as diaphragmatic or belly breathing or internally repeating a soothing word (such as peace or calm) can alleviate stress. As can visualising tranquil scenes. Physical activities are also helpful in preventing and reducing stress – taking a brisk walk shortly after feeling stressed not only deepens breathing but also helps relieve muscle tension. Movement therapies such as yoga, tai chi, and qi gong combine fluid movements with deep breathing and mental focus, all of which can induce calm.

During stressful times your relationship may become strained. It's important that you work together as a team and remind yourself of the strengths that each of you brings to your relationship as a whole.

"Where your thinking goes energy and behavior flows."

– Jacqui Christie

Thoughts of your partner

I want you to think about the type of thoughts you have about your partner. Your thoughts can have an indirect effect on your relationship. Thinking about your partner in a particular way will unconsciously guide you to communicate and behave toward your partner in that particular way. If you are thinking about your partner in an aggressive or angry way, when you next meet them those thoughts are going to come out in some form or another.

In the section of seven principles the first principle I used was the analogy of the garden as your relationship. If you have doubtful or distrustful thoughts about your partner, these become the weeds that need pulling out in the garden. If you constantly tell yourself that your partner does not really love or care for you this is reinforcing those same thoughts inside of you and also becomes a weed that needs dealing with. And if you are thinking your partner will never ever change this too is a weed. Over time these weeds or negative thoughts can take hold in your mind and become a strong belief that grows over the other things your partner may be doing or saying.

If you think of times when your partner may have tried to reach out to you or may have shown you kindness or understanding, you are planting seeds in your mind. Perhaps you can think about the times when you really felt trust with your partner or the times when you felt the safest with them.

If you allow yourself to think about the different ways your partner adds to your life and enriches your experience again you are planting seeds of positivity into your mind. These are the kinds of seeds that will enable you to feel closer and more connected to your partner.

One of my favourite sayings is *"Focus on what you want, not on what you don't want"* –this is particularly important in terms of your relationship. If you focus your thoughts and attention on the kind of relationship you want to have (instead of all the things that you think are lacking) you will notice that you begin to feel very different toward your partner.

"If you keep doing what you're doing you'll keep getting what you get."

– Jacqui Christie

Mindful communication

The gentle words below are an excerpt from Thich Nhat Hanh's interpretation of the Buddhist Fourth Precept. Thich Nhat Hanh is a Vietnamese monk, renowned Zen master, poet and peace activist. The vow below talks of avoiding false speech of all kinds, and is used as a reminder and guidance to anyone who is interested in following mindfulness.

I have presented it here as an example of a guiding principle in how to behave toward yourself and your partner.

> *Aware of the suffering caused by un-mindful speech and the inability to listen to others, I vow to cultivate loving speech and deep listening in order to bring joy and happiness to others and relieve others of their suffering.*
>
> *Knowing that words can create happiness or suffering, I vow to learn to speak truthfully, with words that inspire self-confidence, joy, and hope.*
>
> *I am determined not to spread news that I do not know to be certain and not to criticize or condemn things of which I am not sure.*
>
> *I will refrain from uttering words that can cause division or discord, or that can cause the family or the community to break.*
>
> *I will make all efforts to reconcile and resolve all conflicts, however small.*

Play together to stay together

When was the last time you and your partner played together? When you did something as a couple that was pure fun, even silliness?

When you get caught up with your day-to-day life it's easy to fall into the trap of just doing what you're doing and not paying attention to what's happening between the two of you in your relationship. Keeping fun and friendship alive in your relationship is one of the most important factors in feeling safe and creating a secure relationship. Recent research has found that the amount of fun couples have together is the strongest factor in overall marital happiness.

So how can you inject some fun into your relationship?

One of the ways is to look for new shared experiences, especially something that is a little different, exciting or novel. The celebrated anthropologist Helen Fisher states that from a biological perspective doing something novel increases the levels of the neurotransmitter dopamine in your brain which is seen as the love drug. Dopamine is linked to the reward circuits in your brain so when you are doing something novel with your partner you feel an intense rush of pleasure; your brain finds it exciting and wants to do it again and again.

Researchers Arthur Aron and his colleagues have tested the effects of novelty on marriage. In one of the earliest studies, 53 middle-aged couples were measured on their relationship quality then randomly assigned to different groups. All groups were instructed to spend 90 minutes a week doing activities. Activities in one group were classified as 'pleasant', like dining out or going to a movie. In the other group activities had to be 'exciting', especially something that appealed to both partners. Examples were activities they didn't usually do like attending concerts or plays, skiing, hiking or dancing. After ten weeks, the couples who had undertaken the 'exciting' activities showed a significantly greater increase in marital satisfaction than the 'pleasant' date night group.

In a more recent laboratory experiment couples were asked to simply walk back and forth across a room. Other couples had their wrists and ankles bound together and had to crawl back and forth across the room pushing a ball. Before and after the exercise, both sets of couples were asked "How bored are you with your current relationship?" The couples who had to walk back and forth across the room showed no changes in their responses. While the couples who took part in the more challenging and novel activity revealed bigger increases in love and satisfaction scores.

Try out your own experiment

Sit down together and choose some novel and or exciting activities you would both like to do as a couple, something that you have not done together before. For the next four weeks deliberately set time aside every other day to implement your fun choices

Remember it doesn't always have to be something that will take hours, it could be a 30-minute activity. So that you can maximise what you both enjoy as fun its best to develop your own unique activities.

Below are some ideas from other couples to get you started:

- Play games like Scrabble, Dominoes, Wii, Uno, Quiddler, Frisbee or Catchphrase.
- Take a walk or run together.
- Have a pillow fight.
- Play hide and seek.
- Go on a trust walk, one person leads the other while blindfolded and then switch.
- Cook together, try new recipes and enjoy a great meal together.
- List activities for each letter of the alphabet that cost less than $10, then work your way through the list.

- Work together on a jigsaw puzzle.
- Do a crossword puzzle together.
- Do activities together like horseback riding, hiking, dancing, fishing or kayaking.

Play isn't a luxury, it's a necessity. Play helps you smooth over the rough patches in your relationship. Instead of reminiscing about how playful and adventurous you used to be or complaining that you never do anything fun anymore, *take action*. Do something different. You will both benefit and enjoy being around each other more.

PART FOUR

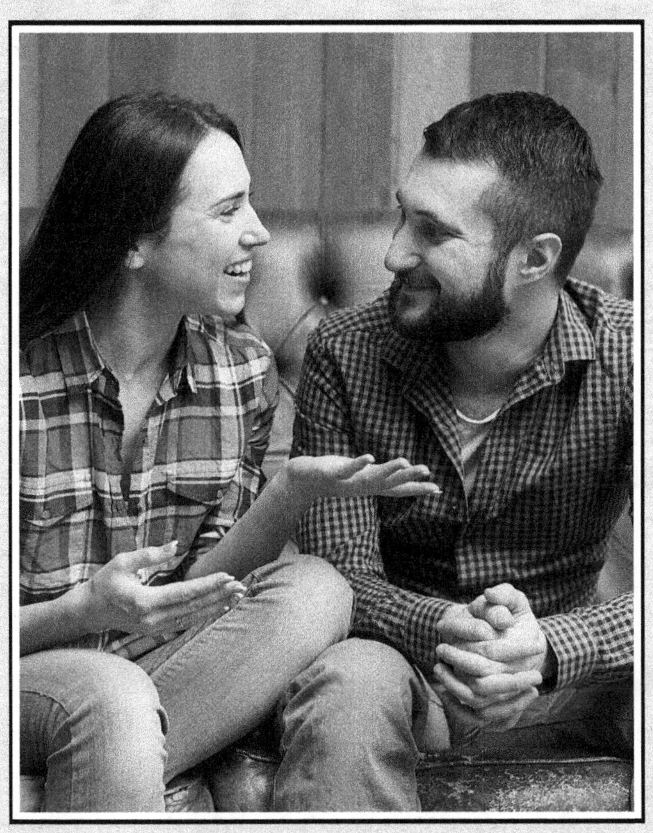

Communication for Commitment

PART FOUR

Communication for Commitment

Belief structures

Your belief system instructs the way the way you think about yourself and others as well as the way you think about your environment. Your beliefs are what you and you alone *perceive* to be *true* (having nothing to do with other peoples' beliefs). They are formed from your perception of an event as well as what is taken in by your senses.

Beliefs are mainly out of your conscious awareness but they form the basis for your thinking, shape your emotional responses and result in actions.

Your beliefs significantly influence the way in which you communicate to your partner. Think of these two common phrases couples use: "You made me do this or that" or "If it wasn't for you I would never have done that"

Even though this is a common way to communicate, in fact no one can make you feel anything that you do not already feel yourself. Let me explain.

When your partner says something you don't like or don't want to hear and you react and defend yourself, what's actually happened is that they have touched on an emotional sensitivity hidden inside you. I liken it to touching an internal bruise that hasn't healed yet. The tricky thing is, you may not even be aware that you hold this sensitivity inside of you. Even if you were aware that doesn't always mean that what you believe about yourself is indeed true (our mind has been known to lie to us). So when that bruise is touched you feel it, its sore and it's painful! No-one wants to feel pain so it's likely you will react to stop that feeling. Because your partner's comment began the process you feel it's their fault and say something along the lines of "You made me feel this way".

The bruise or sensitivity that you carry within may be something someone said about you years ago when you were very young or it may have been an experience at school that you have pushed down so far in your memory that you have forgotten. This is where it can get even more complicated. Because it's from such a long time ago it becomes embedded in your brain, it becomes part of the belief structure that you hold inside, and it becomes your truth! My guess is it's probably not true at all it's actually something that you have been told about yourself from somebody that was in emotional pain too and had also been told something untrue about themselves. And so it goes on through the generations.

We can see through this type of scenario how negative attention can impact the development of the social and emotional part of the brain. If in the early parts of your life you were consistently told that you were clumsy, stupid, or not good at something then don't be surprised if it becomes an internal belief for you, a truth that you carry around in your head.

When you're a child you haven't fully developed so you don't know who you are yet. One of the ways you develop your personality is through what other people tell you about yourself. Your primary attachment figures are often the first people to tell you these kinds of things and they begin to define you. As a child you were like a little sponge soaking up everything you saw, heard and were told so you easily took on these definitions and ideas yourself and they became embedded in your mind.

As a young child you were not in a position to question, let alone challenge what your primary attachment figures said about you. So instead you unconsciously took on and applied the definitions of yourself that they gave you. If they were negative definitions, you tell yourself you're not good at X or can't do Y well. Because your caregivers said this about you, it must be true.

On the other end of the spectrum you may have been told you were pretty, clever, athletic, creative, intelligent, hard

worker or any number of positive traits. The same process applies. It's likely you have some positive and some negative definitions of yourself embedded as part of your beliefs.

In thousands of different ways, both subtly and overtly, your parents gave you the message that they approved of only specific parts of you. Those early definitions or labels became an unconscious part of your belief system and can stay around for as long as you live. Some of your beliefs can get in the way of having the relationship you desire. So it's in both you and your partner's interests to think about what some of those deep-seated beliefs could be that you have never questioned. Through this process, you can start to unravel and understand how you came to take on that particular belief about yourself.

Triangulation

Do you remember the saying 'two's company, three's a crowd'? It's a pretty old one and used by lovers who wanted to be by themselves as a couple. The inclusion of another person would make them feel more self-conscious with each other. If we look at your current relationship, this old saying has influences in ways you are probably not aware of.

The concept of Triangulation comes from the family systems theorist Murray Bowen. Bowen believed that when a couple have to deal with stress within their relationship it becomes unstable and it is common to pull someone or something else in to relieve the stress. If a third party is drawn in, the focus shifts to criticising or worrying about the new outsider, which in turn prevents the couple from resolving their tension.

When the two of you are attuned or in balance with each other you are able to meet each other's needs and function well. Triangulation can become unhealthy in relationships when it causes undue stress on the third party and/or when it prevents, the resolution of your conflicts.

Triangulation can happen with anything that demands a fair amount of attention from only one of you. A triangle can be many different things. It can be a TV show your partner watches alone instead of with you. It can be your car, computer or your phone. The hobby that you or your partner enjoys and the amount of time it takes away from the time you could be spending with each other. Your pets that love you unconditionally and are allowed on your bed every night. And what of your work and how you convince yourself that you really have to spend extra time there, because everyone else does, or so you are not overlooked for that promotion or pay rise.

It's important to keep individuality in your relationship, and enjoy your own hobbies and friends, but that must be balanced against keeping your relationship as the priority. Your partner needs to feel that they are first in your life, which in turn, allows you the freedom to do the things you would like to do.

There are many outside influences that can get in the way of a relationship sometimes because they have to and sometimes accidentally. You can't always control what happens but you can manage how you both deal with them when they arise.

Triangulation can become a threat to your relationship if you or your partner becomes overly involved in whatever that triangle is. Your relationship can become marginalised in favour of that triangle. If one or both of you are feeling like other things are more important to your partner than you, this will disrupt your relational safety and security system and the unconscious desire you both have for security and love.

A subtle and common way that triangles can creep into your relationship is if you have children. Many couples focus more on the children than the relationship. This is understandable as your children are dependent on you and your partner is an adult. However, even though your children are very significant in your lives it's more important for them to see you behave lovingly toward each other. To show them how you and your partner are connected to each other and work as a team. It's important in your family that neither one of you feels replaced nor sidelined in your relationship even if it's by your children. You need a strong relationship to parent well and teach your kids by example what a secure and stable family is all about.

The Ultimate Triangle

The ultimate triangle is of course an affair. It is without a doubt the biggest and most dangerous in any relationship. Dangerous in terms of the threat it poses to your relationship. If you have ever experienced this first-hand, then you know what I'm talking about. Affairs can begin quite innocently especially with that person who is just so easy to talk to and is always concerned for your wellbeing. The more you confide in that person the less you will share with your partner. It is your partner that you want to develop your relationship with so turning to another person for that connection effectively sidelines your partner, creating a rupture in the safety and security of your relationship.

How to manage Triangulation

You as a couple have a limited amount of internal energy with which to care for one another and your relationship. When this energy is spent in areas outside the relationship, your relationship can be compromised. To maintain the energy between the two of you place each other at the top of the pecking order in the family. You are the king and queen of your domain and everyone else are the citizens. This includes your family and children. Implementing this idea creates a strong foundation for your relationship and gives your children the best security blanket they will ever have.

Make an agreement that no other people or things are allowed into the relationship unless both of you agree. Other influences are kept as close or as far away as you both decide.

Your work, friends, extended family, hobbies, outdoor shed or housework cannot become more important than the two of you.

Triangulation can be used in a positive way to help build your relationship when you interact together as a couple with the triangle. For example, watching TV together, during the adverts press mute and talk to each other about what's happening in the show. If going somewhere together, don't drift off on into your own thoughts or get lost in the activity. Instead talk to each other about what you feel, see or hear about what you are doing together.

If something wonderful happens to you, like a promotion, a pregnancy confirmation, or any other good news share this with your partner first. Develop mutual hobbies or activities like gardening, travelling, snowboarding or spending time with family and friends.

You can ensure that your relationship is strong by keeping triangles where they belong. If you have said to people that nothing is more important than your partner, then take action and show your partner how they are the most important person in your life.

Exercise:

Write a list of the things that you know are triangles in your relationship. Ask your partner to do the same.

Compare your lists and discuss with each other.

Using some of the suggestions above talk about where you can each make adjustments in your relationship. e.g. shared time versus individual time.

"Our beliefs shape our perceptions."

– Jacqui Christie

Fighting Fair – Heal your relationship and heal your heart

It is unrealistic to think that you will never fight with your partner or that you can avoid having arguments. Conflicts and fights are absolutely normal in a relationship and all couples will disagree and fight from time to time.

Many couples who come to relationship therapy or couples counselling say that they are coming because of communication issues. It could be that they are not communicating at all or it could be that they start out by having a discussion with their partner about something but then get

lost somewhere along the way and end up arguing. Other common topics tend to be around financial issues, struggling with balancing the chequebook due to a variety of reasons. When one partner is away from the home a considerable length of time in the evenings or days away, time becomes the issue that is brought to the table. Children are another important topic couple's often struggle with, whether it's coping with stepchildren or the couple's own children and this can often lead into another popular concern, which is mess. This could be mess from the children or from one or the other partner. And last but not least is the topic of sex which is usually to do with one person wanting to engage in more sexual activity than their partner.

What I would like you to know that even though the above topics are the most common areas that may bring a couple to counselling NONE of these topics is actually the REAL issue. The underlying or real issue is the lack of intimacy between you and your partner. When I refer to a lack of intimacy I'm not talking just about the sexual kind, although that is important, what I'm talking about is a lack of connection between you and your partner, a misreading of each other's cues, where one goes left the other goes right, a *misattunement*.

Misattunement with your partner is that feeling of being at odds with each other, feeling not quite right or that something is off but you're not sure what it is, or not being on the same page with each other. It is misattunement that can get you both into trouble and create an argument. It is important that you pay attention to these small moments of missed connection and attend to them as soon as possible. Repairing quickly creates that feeling of security and will also ensure that you have fewer arguments.

However for those inevitable times when you argue you might notice that arguments often occur through small or large misunderstandings with each other. How often have you heard your friends or your partner, or even yourself say "You are just doing this to upset me" or "Why would you continue after I have made it crystal clear that I don't want you to do that?". This example is where some couples are not able to understand what their partner's intentions are, or worse, believe that their partner's intentions are to deliberately harm them.

Sometimes it might appear like an argument has come out of the blue. You may find that neither of you has any idea what happened as you didn't notice anything obvious prior to the argument. Conflict can arise because of a gradual build-up of small or irritating occurrences. The gradual build-up can be over one day or over a number of days and weeks. This kind of behaviour is more prevalent if either of you have an avoidant attachment style. If you are focussed on keeping the peace or trying to keep everyone happy and want people

to like you, it's probable that you may try to avoid or ignore irritating comments. Sometimes you may not even be aware that comments or situations bother you but it's often the case that these incidents are still sitting in your unconscious mind whether you're aware of it or not.

Another situation is the feeling of going from 0–100 in a short period of time, from calm to furious anger. This reminds me of the saying 'the straw that broke the camel's back' and it's likely this is exactly what has happened. Once again small things have irritated or annoyed you and been ignored or pushed aside. Your partner may say something inconsequential like can you pick up your shoes and whoops... that poor camel's back gets broken! It can be over the day or week or even months that all of those small things have accumulated inside you and all it takes is one more thing to tip you over the edge. However, your partner doesn't know this and they have only made a reasonable request for you to pick up your shoes. So how do you become aware earlier and how do you manage these small irritants? How do you know what's really going on?

Knowing what's happening physiologically is one of the steps to reduce conflict. You can start to recognise the early signs and signals your body is sending you. You may already be able to notice some external signs, for example clenching your fists or tightness in your arms. You will however experience a number of other physical and behavioural cues that you can use to become aware of your irritation or agitation.

Physiological and behavioural signs of agitation and anger can include:

- tension in your head
- rubbing your head
- feeling hot
- light headedness or dizziness
- increased and rapid heart rate
- acting in an abusive or abrasive manner
- clenching your teeth
- raising your voice
- grinding your teeth
- stomach ache
- sweating, especially your palms
- shaking or trembling
- behaving in an irritable or agitated way
- becoming sarcastic
- losing your sense of humour
- craving any substance that relaxes you

It's really important to pay attention to any sensations you notice or feel in your body. This is a practice that will assist you well before your amygdalae becomes activated. The sooner you notice any sensations the sooner and earlier you are able to do something about it.

"Remember this is the person you LOVE."

– Jacqui Christie

Fight or flight and the rise of the lizard brain

Working on how you fight is more important than what you fight about. Fighting fair is about how you manage conflict. Couples expert Stan Tatkin believes that even on the best day our communication is really bad (Tatkin 2013). When you are feeling okay with each other and are having a good day you let things go more easily. But when you are not feeling okay with each other you become very aware of how much misattunement between you really occurs. This causes your biological system to become hyperactivated, moving you into the fight or flight response. It is the amygdalae that are responsible for that response, and is the first part of your biological threat system to become activated. The amygdalae are named for their small shape and size and are the Greek name for almonds. They are one of our most primitive brain structures and are sometimes called the lizard brain, as they are always on alert. The main purpose of the amygdalae is as a watchdog or overseer of the brain, constantly scanning for danger or threat. They are easily tripped off by perceptions that appear frightening or scary. Such perceptions can be words or movements, or even body postures or tone of voice. When your amygdalae are activated you and your partner begin to behave like predators toward each other and you will say and do things that you would never do whilst not in that activated state. Your threat response is so deep-seated that it works faster than you or your partner can even think. This is because threatening experiences become encoded more strongly in your memory than non-threatening experiences (Cassidy & Shaver 2016).

As soon as you or your partner are perceived as frightening, your biological threat systems take over which prevents either of you from achieving the outcome you are hoping for. It is incredibly easy to make yourself sound or look dangerous or scary to your partner. Behaviours like eye-rolling, grunting, tutting, sighing, looking down your nose, disdain, showing contempt or disgust all send signals to your partner that you are unfriendly. Using harmful words or phrases do the same thing. Harmful words and behaviours signal to your partner's amygdalae that you are threat and therefore need to be defended against or avoided at all costs.

Transference and conflict

When you are arguing with your partner you are not just arguing with your partner. Huh??? Let me explain – you are in fact arguing with all the people in your past that had similarities to your partner and the way in which your partner argues now. Even if their behaviour isn't similar you will unconsciously transfer feelings from your past relationships onto the present one. "Why would I want to do that?" I hear you saying... Well, essentially because you want to resolve the early conflicts or struggles you experienced with your primary attachment figures or early love relationships, with your current partner.

For the most part this is all out of your awareness. Even more confused? I'm not surprised. This happens because of two major things are occurring in your brain, autopilot and transference.

Autopilot

Whether you are aware of it or not, your brain is on autopilot most of the time. *Autopilot* or habitual learning is the reason you can drive somewhere and disturbingly not recall the process of getting there. It's also the explanation for some forms of multitasking you do, like eating and driving, or walking and talking on the phone. When you learn something new like driving a car you are using two different parts of your brain, one part is responsible for movement and the other part for higher cognition. As you eventually learn a task, the cognitive part of the brain is used less in favour of the movement part, which is strengthened. You are then able to continue doing the task with very little thinking if at all, hence autopilot. Being on autopilot can be useful in some activities, however when it's applied to your relationship, and more importantly to conflict with your partner, you are going to run into a number of difficulties.

Transference

Transference is the idea of unconsciously redirecting or transferring feelings, fears or wishes from the past onto the present. The theory was developed by Sigmund Freud, the founder of psychoanalysis. It is a universal phenomenon that is automatic and unconscious and something that most people do in their lives. Remember your relational template? How it recorded and stored hundreds of interactions in your brain, both positive and negative with your primary attachment figures and other important people in your life?. When it comes to conflicts and other uncomfortable feelings, your brain unconsciously pulls forward some of those interactions and superimposes them over whatever is happening in the moment. Imagine it like a filter over the top of what's really going on. This is largely because you unconsciously assume that if you re-enact conflict, there is a good chance of it being resolved because again unconsciously you assign the role of parent to your partner. Your partner becomes your substitute primary attachment figure so sometimes you will act out toward them with the hope that they will respond differently toward you and heal some of those lingering hurts.

It takes a lot of awareness, and I mean *a lot* of awareness, to notice when this is occurring and especially when your amygdalae have been triggered off.

Why is this important to my relationship?

When you and your partner automatically relate to each other based on your past experiences and unconsciously restage memories of conflicts as if the past were the present, you are more likely to go off track in your arguments. You are more

likely to bring up topics that are not even remotely related to what you are arguing about. You are more likely to feel even more pain than usual when in conflict because those pasts wounds are so deeply embedded in your psyche.

The reason it's important to understand why you automatically do this is so you can work toward minimising the emotional damage transference and autopilot do to your relationship.

It is up to you to work toward making the unconscious conscious.

So, what can you do to de-escalate and change each other's emotional state?

Calming down your amygdalae

- Notice your bodily warning signals
- Sit down. Standing up is threatening to your partner
- Face each other while arguing. Continue facing each other and do not look away
- Look into your partner's eyes. Holding your partner's gaze stops your brain from going back into a memory of another time
- Pay attention to each other's vocal, facial and bodily cues
- Shock your brain and say "I love you" in the middle of conflict
- Don't make quick jerky movements, like waving your arms around

- Remember to breathe. Holding your breath or shallow breathing activates the fight or flight reaction
- Relax your breathing slowly breathing in to the count of three and breathing out to the count of five. It is important not to take in large gulps of air as you will most likely become hyper-aroused
- Be friendly. Smile, yes smile at your partner
- Apologise to your partner, even if you don't think you need to
- Agree with you partner, even if you really don't
- Pause. Ask each other if you really want to be doing this right now
- Take a break. Stop arguing and both make a commitment to return and discuss later when calmer.

Exercise:

Ask yourself these questions and write down the answers on a piece of paper then share with each other.

When I am arguing with my partner:

- What thoughts do I have when my partner acts this way?
- How do I feel when my partner acts this way?
- What deeper feelings might underlie these thoughts and feelings?
- When and what was my earliest memory of these same thoughts and feelings?

Fighting fair with an avoidant

If you have discovered that your partner has an avoidant attachment style, they are likely to experience conflict as a threat to the relationship. There are a few key points that can help you modify the way you manage your argument.

One of the most essential points is that your avoidant partner will avoid conflict in a big way. In fact, your partner will do anything in their power to avoid having an argument. Your partner struggles with conflict because it is interpreted as a threat to your attachment together. Remember you are both operating as each other's primary attachment figures so any signs of conflict unconsciously trigger this feeling off.

Your avoidant partner is also likely to have a more passive communication style, often using long rambling sentences to express themselves. They may beat around the bush and not get to the point of what they are trying to say. Your partner may not express their feelings thoughts or beliefs and if they do, express them in an apologetic, meek way. This style allows other people to often disregard what they have to say. Although they will try to stay away from conflict as much as possible, if they are very angry they will become involved. Once involved their behaviour becomes very quiet and still and they will let you do most of the talking. Whilst they may appear to be listening to you they are actually attempting to regulate their emotions as they are feeling overwhelmed.

Your partner may have a smile on their face, but this is yet another way to manage the emotional stress building inside them. If they do speak out it is often with a sarcastic or passive aggressive tone, with something that can humiliate you and stop you in your tracks or cut you off at the knees. This type of behaviour is often used as a last resort and is more to do with your partner's unconscious desire to stop the conflict.

Remember your partner's early attachment experience has really not prepared them for intense displays of emotion. So conflict, or even the perception of conflict, poses an enormous threat to your avoidant partner and, they will cope by deactivating the attachment system between you. They will withdraw or downplay the significance of the conflict and you. This may look like they are not interested in the argument or indeed anything you have to say. They may dismiss your concerns out of hand and in some cases this is literally with a wave of their hand.

Using the above information and coming from an informed place of understanding

- Ask yourself how important is it that you both have a win–win outcome
- Make a prior agreement to cut the argument short if either of you becomes hyper-activated
- Regulate your breathing

- Talk calmly and quietly to your partner
- Use assertive communication
- Be aware of and sensitive toward your partner
- Notice changes in your partner's facial expressions
- Stop talking if your partner looks overwhelmed
- Don't use your partner's vulnerabilities against them
- If your partner walks away or leaves the argument do not pursue them.

Fighting fair with an ambivalent

If your partner has an ambivalent style, any form of conflict is likely to trigger concerns about being abandoned by you. You are both each other's surrogate primary caregiver and your partner unconsciously interprets conflict as a sign that the relationship is ending.

There are a few key points to help you modify the way you manage the conflict.

Because your ambivalent partner is very expressive when they are in an argument, they may become angry and even aggressive. Your partner could yell, scream and swear and may try to intimidate you by getting up in your face, pointing their finger at you or even poking you. Threats are a large part of their conflict repertoire and they will threaten to do a number of dramatic things including leave the relationship in a variety of ways. This happens because their attachment insecurities have been hyper-activated as well as their amygdala. I know this may sound strange but your ambivalent partner wants connection with you. They want you to understand and validate them but they already believe it's not going to happen, that you will let them down and disappoint them just as they were disappointed as a child. At this stage you may not have done anything to let them down but they are convinced you are going to. Part of their unconscious attachment template tells them "I'm going to get angry at you before you have any chance to let me down". One of the problems with arguing with your ambivalent partner is that they don't know how to stop an argument so will keep it going endlessly. They get stuck in rehashing unresolved situations and will go round and round in a loop or a repetitive pattern of old hurts and wounds.

One woman I knew who was ambivalent was in a relationship with an avoidant man. Every time they had an argument, she would grab all her clothes and throw them into a suitcase, then run out of the door screaming that she did not need to put up with this anymore and that she was out of here! She would jump into the car and screech off, only to drive around for about 30 to 45 minutes, stop the car and fall into a heap crying with desperation. She repeated this behaviour for many years, as if trying to get her partner to change his

response toward her. She truly believed that the threat of her leaving would make her partner come after her would make him see how important she was to him. Of course her partner, being an avoidant, never did come after her. Over time he did begin to call her and text her, concerned about her safety and to check if she was okay.

Because your ambivalent partner struggles with managing their own emotions, they will look to you to reassure or soothe them. Their anger and aggression is a defence to protect them from being hurt, so it's likely that if you attempt to approach them they will push you away. If you can see past the prickly thorns on the outside, on the inside there is often a mass of softness just waiting to be soothed.

Using the above information and coming from an informed place of understanding,

- Ask yourself how important is it that we both have a win/win outcome
- Be aware and sensitive toward your partner
- Do not take anything said personally
- Remind yourself what is going on is not directed at you
- Maintain eye contact
- Regulate your breathing
- Slowly approach your partner

- Open your arms
- Give them a hug
- Speak softly in a low tone
- Tell them you're not going anywhere.

You may or may not believe this right now, but the person who knows you the most is actually your partner. The majority of things you argue about have to do with your attachment histories. You may believe it's to do with something your partner did or didn't do but the reality is you are both unconsciously relating to each other as your primary caregiver. Once you start to fully understand your attachment patterns you will be amazed at just how much is related to those patterns and how much is NOT about your partner. Just knowing that can relieve so much tension from your relationship.

Win–Win Communication

Aggressive and assertive communication

Communication is one of the areas that can cause the most friction between couples. So understanding how you both communicate can help you make conscious choices to improve your methods and create a win–win outcome for you and your partner. Depending on what form of language you were raised with and what the common way of communicating

was between your primary attachment figures, you will tend to lean toward one form or the other.

There are generally two distinct styles of communicating, especially when you are attempting to express your discomfort or anger. These are the aggressive and assertive communication styles. In my experience as a PACT couple's therapist I have found that many people are not aware that there are different styles or they are unsure or confused about the difference between the two. Perhaps this is because what we are really talking about is the difference between aggressive and assertive communication styles.

'You' messages, such as "You made me feel" or "You always talk too much" are classified as an aggressive form and 'I' messages such as "I feel sad" or "I enjoy talking" are viewed as the assertive form of communicating. 'You' messages are a harsh beginning to a conversation and assign blame to the listener, whereas language beginning with 'I' is more inviting to your partner, but also shows you are responsible for what you are talking about.

'You' messages

'You' messages are one the most common ways of communicating between couples –especially, if you feel angry or hurt by something your partner has said. This is when you tell your partner where they have gone wrong or what they should or shouldn't have done.

Let's say you are feeling hurt or resentful at something your partner has said, done or not done. If you begin your communication with the word 'You', as in "You never listen to me" or, "You should pay attention" or even "You need to understand my position", your partner's arousal system becomes hyper-activated and they will feel defensive toward you. This defensiveness can come out as hostility toward what you have said and creates an increased likelihood that your partner will come back at you with another 'You' statement. Most of your partner's energy will be directed toward protecting themselves instead of leaning forward and listening.

Another effect of using the word 'You' is it will emotionally shut them down, whether it's slightly or completely. Your partner may be looking straight at you but may feel unable or unwilling to be open with you and truly listen. It can almost seem like the lights are on but no one is home.

The use of the word 'You' suggests a judgment, and we all know no one likes to be judged, especially by their partner. 'You' statements sound accusatory and blaming, because they are based on assumptions. Even though you may categorically believe that you know exactly what your partner is feeling, thinking or behaving, the reality is that you don't. That's why it's important not to say things like "You don't love me" or "You don't understand me" or "You never do this or that". At

best what's operating here is only your perspective of your partner and at worst it is plain guesswork. More so, the use of such statements means you are not acknowledging or taking responsibility for your own feelings and behaviour.

"Express what you are truly feeling so that it doesn't sneak out in a distorted way."

– Jacqui Christie

'I' messages

The term 'I' messages was developed in the 1960s when they were introduced in Parent Effectiveness Training (PET). 'I' messages are a great way of diffusing or heading off a potential conflict. Stating what you feel instead of what you think is really hard to argue against, because you are coming from your own experience and not blaming your partner. Your partner will hear it as an appeal for help from you instead of an attack. 'I' messages are a very powerful way of co-creating healing communication.

If you notice you are moving toward a potential conflict or your partner has recently hurt you with what they have said, use the words "I feel" and describe your actual feelings. When you talk to your partner using 'I' messages you are acknowledging and taking responsibility for your emotions. Expressing what you feel allows you and your partner to understand your emotions and also helps to make those emotions clearer to both of you. By stating your feelings you are sharing a slightly more open side of yourself to your partner, which in turn enables your partner to experience empathy for you and assists them to have a greater understanding of who you are. Expressing your emotion instead of your perspective allows your partner to relax, lean in and listen to you more. Finally, 'I' messages are non-threatening communication and thereby are viewed as assertive communication.

'I messages' look like this:

- I feel... (insert feeling word)
- When... (say what caused the feeling)
- And I would like... (say what you would like to happen instead).

For example: "I feel unappreciated when I think I'm not being heard. I would like us to look at each other when we talk". Or, "I am feeling unloved and would like to be taken care of more".

It's very common to misunderstand this technique and use it incorrectly. For example hiding the 'You' inside the 'I' message such as "I feel like you don't spend any time with me" or "I feel you're getting angry." Notice that there is no

feeling word or explanation of what has caused the feeling, instead the use of the words "I feel" has the same accusatory effect as 'You' messages.

A couple of other guidelines to remember:

- Always describe the other person's behaviour in a non-blameful or non-judgmental way
- Describe HOW that behaviour has affected you
- Talk about the feelings you have experienced about the behaviour.

Try this out with your partner. If you're worried or anxious about using this technique or concerned about how your partner will hear you, one idea is to first try it out with someone who is not threatening or challenging to you. This could be a trusted family member or friend. Once you have built up your confidence, begin to use it with your partner. This ensures you give yourself the opportunity of maximum success in practising something new, which then enables you to feel more comfortable to make an attempt with your partner.

"Ensure what you say matches how you look and how you feel."

– Jacqui Christie

A word on body language

Ensure your body language and other nonverbal cues match your assertive language. Be aware of how you hold your body, your facial expressions and your tone of voice as body language is also an important part of communication.

If your body and nonverbal cues are different to the words you are saying, you are sending mixed signals to your partner. Mixed signals may undermine the effectiveness of your assertive message.

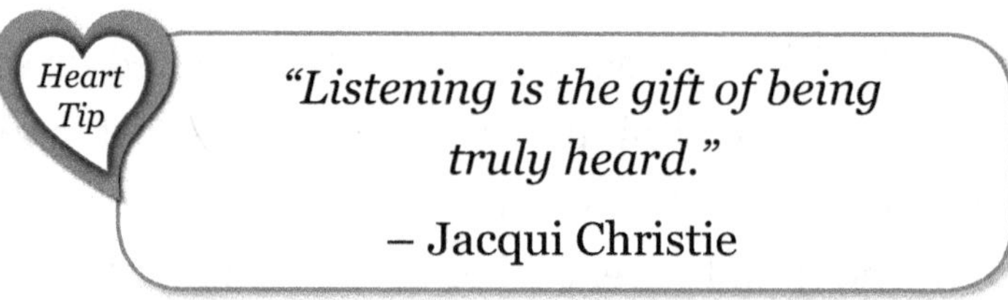

Heart Tip
"Listening is the gift of being truly heard."
– Jacqui Christie

Deep listening

Part of great communication is listening. In fact, in the ten rules of good communication number one is 'stop talking' and number ten is 'stop talking'. If you stop talking you are then able to listen to what your partner is saying. Perhaps you have noticed that your communication doesn't always follow that pattern.

Often we think that listening is a passive, static activity. In fact, deep listening brings about a greater internal awareness

of oneself. Deep listening is a mindful practice and comes from the idea of listening to someone with compassion. It is a way of listening to your partner where you are fully present with what is happening in the moment without trying to control it or judge it. Your focus is on listening to what your partner is saying without interrupting, voicing your opinion or offering advice.

When your partner is talking are you thinking about what you are going to say next, planning your answer or wishing they would just hurry up? Perhaps you interrupt your partner mid-sentence or they interrupt you? If this is what's happening, it means your focus of attention is caught on the surface meaning of the words, rather than listening for what is below the surface.

If you are listening deeply, you are keeping an open and inquisitive mind and being genuinely interested in what you are hearing, or trying to understand where your partner is coming from and what is motivating their speech. You are offering your partner something special: the gift of being truly heard.

When you offer deep listening to your partner you are creating a space for them to hear themselves talk, which leads them to a greater understanding of their own thoughts and feelings. The practice of deep listening allows you to notice any emotions that arise in yourself sooner, enabling you to stop before you say or do something you may later regret. There is then less likelihood that you will trigger a negative reaction in your partner.

Because you are a couple you will both automatically start to synchronise with each other's behaviour, allowing each other to be more at ease and present. You are also creating trust in the process of communication, enabling your partner to trust that regardless of how well or poorly they say something their experience will be validated. You give your partner the opportunity to speak.

A word on tone

Your choice of language is powerful. How you speak to your partner can offer them joy, happiness, self-confidence, hope and trust in you. Plan to use kind speech and choose your words carefully. Become aware of *how* you speak to your partner, especially the tone of voice you use. Choosing soothing tones will draw your partner to you and allow them to lean into you for more.

"Listen with only one purpose to help your partner empty their heart."

– Jacqui Christie

Active listening exercise

This exercise is designed to strengthen how you listen and communicate with each other. Initially it may seem slightly unnatural to do and will require some effort from both of you. The benefit will be that you develop deep listening skills and break the cycle of missed communication.

You will need a timer.

First practise this exercise by talking about something fairly benign or unimportant to your relationship.

Decide who is going to begin as the speaker and who will be the listener. You will be swapping over so it's not important who starts.

Set the timer for three minutes. The statement from the speaker is to last no more than this time. This means the speaker must gather their thoughts, be precise and succinct.

The speaker then states what they want to say. The listener listens, this means no interrupting, commenting, facial expressions or challenging what is being said. Simply listening.

The listener then repeats to the speaker to the best of their ability what they have just heard, ending with the question "Was that correct?" When the listener repeats what they have

heard it must be repeated verbatim, without interpretation or embellishments, exactly as it was spoken.

The speaker then answers the listener with "Yes, that's correct" or "No, that's not correct".

If the response is "No" the listener asks the speaker "Can you repeat it, please?". Now they can listen again and repeat it back again.

If the response is "Yes, that's correct", you can swap and the listener becomes the speaker and continues on with the discussion. The new speaker is also timed for three minutes.

You cannot move on in the discussion until you have repeated back correctly to the speaker what they have said. This means that both of you have to listen to what was being said.

This exercise initially may seem a little clunky and awkward, however it slows both of you down to a point where you can actually listen in small bites what your partner is saying.

It takes practise to truly listen to your partner and hear what they are trying to say.

Once you have practiced active listening together to the point you can actually listen deeply to each other, you can start to introduce other more advanced techniques such as mirroring or paraphrasing.

Mirroring

Mirroring is very similar to active listening except it tends to allow the conversation to flow a little more easily. When you are reflecting back what you have heard you repeat the key words your partner has said or the last few words spoken. Using mirroring shows the speaker you are listening to them as you are using their words. This encourages the speaker to continue. An example can be: "So you're saying it's been really hard for you lately", or "It sounds like it's been really hard for you lately".

Please do not attempt mirroring unless you both agree you already communicate well and or with active listening. Without practise, mirroring can come across as slightly repetitive and the original meaning of what was being said can easily become lost.

Paraphrasing

Paraphrasing is the next stage of communication skills where you use different words to reproduce what the speaker has said. Paraphrasing focuses on the meaning of the topic and allows both of you to achieve greater clarity around what is being spoken. It is really important that you pay attention to what your partner is saying so you can put it into your own words.

This is not the time for you to question how your partner is feeling, or what their behaviour or thoughts are. It is also not the time to introduce your own ideas. It is the time, however, to be open non-judgmental and non-directive in your responses. You are simply using your own words to describe back to your partner the meaning of what they have just said. The meaning is the most important part of paraphrasing and has to be maintained. If this happens greater clarity will be achieved by both of you as you are showing your partner you are attempting to understand what they are saying.

It may sound easy to paraphrase but remember you also have to deal with your autopilot and transference mechanisms which contain the many assumptions you have about your partner being carried around in your brain.

You will definitely need to practice this skill in order to feel comfortable. Initially when you use this with your partner you may feel your communication is clunky and stilted but the more you practise the easier it will become. Who knows, it may even end up being a natural part of your communication style.

There is nothing more powerful to your partner than feeling understood. Using this technique shows your partner that you truly 'get them'.

"Always be curious about your partner."

– Jacqui Christie

The curious enquirer

This is another communication and listening technique that can be used on its own or combined with others. This technique is one of my all-time favourites as it's very simple to learn and when used comes across as easy, genuine and is unnoticeable. It can also have the effect of moving your conversation to a deeper level. Essentially you use a very particular type of enquiry to enquire, and ask your partner for more information about the topic. You enquire even if you think you know the answer to whatever is being discussed. Of course, you enquire in normal conversation if you needed clarification, however this can be used as a specific communication technique.

There are specific responses which prompt the speaker and the conversation to continue and expand. Here are some examples:

... I'm curious to know how that works

... I'm not sure I understand

... Can you help me understand?

... Can you tell me more?

... Hmmmm, I'm wondering what that means

These curious enquiries draw your partner out and help them tell you more about their topic. Using this technique

also helps you learn to listen more effectively and you may discover that what you thought was the problem was not the problem at all.

I am aware that some people are convinced they don't need to draw their partner out because they already know what their partner is thinking. If you are one of those people, then this is definitely the technique for you. Why? Because no one can know exactly what their partner is thinking or actually read their partner's mind.

Although the aim of these exercises is to understand your partner, it is important to never assume anything, because you could be wrong. You can make assumptions, jump to conclusions and judge your partner for certain habits because you know better than them. When you assume that you know what's coming next, for example, your partner may not even say a word and you have already decided what they are going to say or what they have already done or are about to do. This is what I call being The Oracle. The Oracle is that time or place in your life where you believe you know everything there is to know about everything. And there is nothing else left to know. It's when you can come up with the answers every time your partner asks you something, or maybe it's your friends or your children. It's also when you and your partner are talking about something and voila you produce the answer. Sound familiar? Phew what a burden that is!

Always being right and knowing everything is EXHAUSTING don't you think? Having to come up with the answers every time you're asked something or talking about something can be so overwhelming. Indeed it can be crushing for many people in relationships.

On the other hand, being curious about your partner cultivates intimacy and allows you the freedom of letting go of always being right. Such freedom can be had by using some of the prompts I listed above. You are aiming for freedom from the burden of being locked into the role of The Oracle.

One important reason to cultivate curiosity is that it helps you to get to know and understand your partner at a deeper level. From a conversational perspective it helps keeps your conversation flowing. There is always something new you can learn from your partner about themselves, and if you lose that curiosity about your partner then what do you have in your relationship? One of my favourite sayings is 'Never Assume' as it reminds me to be curious about the people I see – perhaps you can use it to jog your memory too.

Heart Tip

"Curiousity cultivates intimacy."

– Jacqui Christie

What will I get out of changing my communication style?

The more you practise your listening and communication skills the more you will notice how different your conversations with your partner will be.

- Your partner will lean in and listen to you more
- You will become more aware of your emotions
- Your partner will become more aware of what you feel
- You will create a more harmonious relationship
- You will move toward creating a win–win conversation

As the renowned therapist Dr John Gottman says, "Happily married couples aren't smarter, richer or more psychologically astute than others. But in their day-to-day lives, they have hit upon a dynamic that keeps their negative thoughts and feelings about each other (which all couples have) from overwhelming their positive ones. They have what I call an Emotionally Intelligent Marriage" (Gottman & Silver 2015).

Love lives in your brain

It's a common belief that feelings of love are associated with your heart. The actuality is a little bit different. Feelings of love are developed in the brain. Researcher Dr Helen Fisher found there are three main stages that you go through when falling in love:

- Lust
- Attraction and
- Attachment.

Chemicals and hormones are produced in the brain and body during these stages and are responsible for and explain why you felt the way you did.

When you fell in love with your partner, your body released a flood of feel-good neuro-chemicals that triggered specific physical reactions. These feel-good chemicals are associated with pleasure and excitement and also with your brain's reward system. The chemicals work together in an elegant way and often overlap and trigger each other.

Lust Stage

Lust is the first stage and is driven by the hormones testosterone and oestrogen. It is these hormones that motivate you to go out seek out a partner and find sexual gratification.

Attraction Stage

When you were first attracted to your partner, a chemical chain of reaction was set off in your brain.

This is the phase when you can really start to feel those feelings we call love. This is also called the passionate stage of being in love.

The chemicals produced are:

- PEA or phenylethylamine – a naturally occurring stimulant responsible for the elated euphoric head-over-heels feelings you had when you first fell in love with your partner. It is also responsible for those early feelings of infatuation that can lead to you feeling almost addicted to your partner.
- Norepinephrine or adrenaline – triggered to release by the PEA in your brain. You'll know when this chemical is in your system when you notice your heart pounding and racing faster and your palms sweating. Interestingly this neurochemical won't become activated if there is not enough dopamine in your system. If you have high levels of norepinephrine in your brain your appetite will be reduced and you have an increased experience of joy. Sound familiar?
- Dopamine – also a neurotransmitter and a natural stimulant that is also triggered by PEA. Dopamine production is responsible for your focused attention, motivation to see your partner and the high feelings of ecstasy you experience. It explains that rush you feel at the sight of your partner and why you may sleep less.
- Serotonin – the chemical responsible for you thinking about your partner and nothing else. It is responsible for the feelings of significance and importance. However serotonin also brings on the feelings of calmness and wellbeing as it

controls impulses and obsessive behaviour, leading you to feel more in control of your emotions.

Attachment Stage

This is the stage that takes over after the attraction phase if your relationship is to last. It is impossible to stay in the attraction stage forever as your brain and body would not be able to cope with that much intensity. The attachment stage is a longer lasting commitment and is the stage where you have a deep understanding of each other and see yourself as life partners. There are two important hormones that are released by your nervous system:

- Oxytocin or the 'cuddle hormone' is released when dopamine has been triggered in your system. Your brain releases oxytocin when you spend time with your partner, in particular touching each other. This is the hormone that is released during orgasm and promotes bonding to each other during intimacy. It tends to stay around longer and is central to encouraging trust, commitment and attachment to your partner.
- Vasopressin also known as the monogamy chemical is produced during a long-term commitment. Vasopressin is responsible for creating the desire by your male partner to stay with only you above all other women. Vasopressin is also found in semen.

A word on endorphins

The feelings of passionate love, however, do lose their strength over time. Studies have shown that passionate love fades quickly and is nearly gone after two or three years. It is during this stage that endorphins begin to be created in your brains.

Endorphins are morphine-like opiates and have quite a different effect on you than the excitement chemicals produced in the attraction phase. Endorphins encourage and build closeness through feelings of intimacy, dependability, warmth and shared experiences. They calm anxiety, relieve pain and reduce stress. The longer you both stay together the more likely you will produce endorphins. Because endorphins are also produced during sex, studies show the more sex you have as a couple, the deeper your bond becomes.

So remember when you thought you had a special chemistry with your partner you were actually right!

PART FIVE

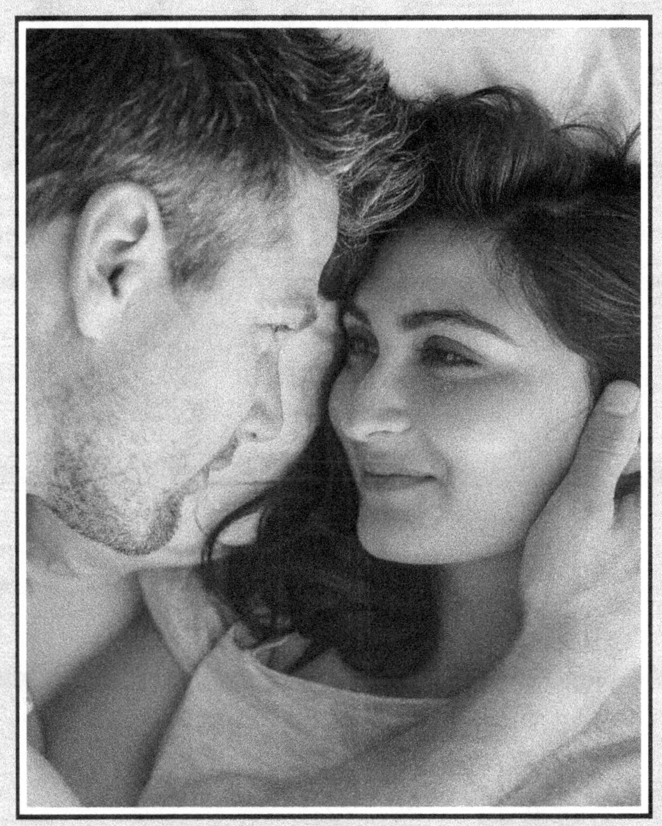

Practices for a Loving Relationship

PART FIVE

Practices for a Loving Relationship

Practices to create a passionate and loving relationship and stoke the fires of love and connection

Passionate love and connection

"I like my body when it is with your
body. It is so quite new a thing.
Muscles better and nerves more.
I like your body. I like what it does,
I like its hows. I like to feel the spine
of your body and its bones, and the trembling
-firm-smooth ness and which I will
again and again and again
kiss, I like kissing this and that of you,
I like, slowly stroking the, shocking fuzz
of your electric furr, and what-is-it come
over parting flesh.... And eyes big love-crumbs,
and possibly I like the thrill
of under me you so quite new"

E. E. Cummings

This poem captures the essence of a deep connection between two people incorporating lust, love and intimacy. You too may have yearned for such a connection in your relationship. Perhaps this is the type of depth that you have long desired to have with your partner. Perhaps you used to have a deep connection and have lost it somewhere along the way.

How do you recreate your relationship and enhance romance in your lives?

This section was designed to assist in creating more love, intimacy, connection and companionship in your relationship. While a couple of the techniques are for you alone the majority are for you and your partner to try out.

Breathing Retraining

In order to allow yourself and your partner to feel more sexually or intimately connected to each other it's essential to give your body the experience of being relaxed.

Breathing exercises have long been one of the ways to initiate physical calmness and relaxation, as well as ensuring a greater physical connection to oneself. We typically do not breathe properly, actually doing more of what researchers call shallow breathing, which entails using only the top half of our lungs instead of using our full lung capacity.

Before you begin, practise breathing in while pushing your stomach out keeping your chest and shoulders stable. Imagine your stomach is like a balloon that you are blowing up. Then slowly release your stomach. Do this a couple of times until you're confident you can push only your stomach out and then release.

Once you have mastered this technique you will begin to notice the benefits in how relaxed your body now feels, which of course leads onto feeling more open to your partner touching, caressing or holding you.

I suggest implementing this exercise in the form of a nightly practice.

Exercise:

Lie down comfortably with both of your hands resting on your stomach with your index fingers touching.

Breathe in through your nose while you push your stomach out. (Notice how your fingers naturally move apart).

Hold your breath for as long as you can while your stomach is pushed out then purse your lips while you blow the air out slowly through your lips. Control the flow of breath outward without allowing it to rush out of your mouth. (Notice how your stomach flattens out as you blow out.)

Relax your breathing for a moment.

Then do the exercise again. Practise this pattern for seven cycles. One cycle consists of breath in, hold, and breathe out.

Practising your breathing retraining every night will not only help you to physically relax but is a great technique should you have difficulty sleeping and wake up during the night.

You may notice a rush to your head during this exercise. This is perfectly normal as your brain is receiving more oxygen than it has previously has. Over time and with practise this will settle down.

After you have mastered this practice you will be able to implement it during the day and will not need to purse your lips but be able to breathe out through your nose.

However, lying down whilst doing this exercise will help assist you to establish this practice.

Five Senses

This is one of my favourite techniques, a brief mindfulness exercise that brings your attention into the present moment. This can be especially helpful if you find your mind is often distracted and your partner needs you to be focussed and attentive to them. Including this exercise in your daily routine will bring you a greater awareness of your immediate surroundings, including all of your senses.

Exercise:

Slowly look around your environment and ask yourself the questions below. When moving through each of the senses, savour each of them for a few moments, not too quick and not too slow. After asking each question, answer in your mind.

- What can I see? (hold your gaze for a few moments) I can see a photo frame
- What can I hear? (take your time to listen) I can hear the birds
- What can I smell? (breathe in deeply so as to notice) I can smell coffee
- What can I taste? (any after taste?) I can taste tomato soup
- What am I touching? (bring your attention to what you're touching) I am touching my hands

Exercise (continued):

This technique can be used in the office, at home or with your in-laws. When you focus on your senses it brings your attention and your mind very quickly into the present moment which allows your mind to pause and not wander off.

The main reason for implementing and practicing this technique is for the benefit of your relationship. It can enable you to feel grounded and present so you can connect more easily to your partner.

"Gaze into your partner's eyes and reconnect."

– Jacqui Christie

Into me see

'Into me see' or gentle gazing is an exercise of looking into each other's eyes for a period of time without speaking. Practising eye-gazing is a simple tool that you can both do to create safety and security in your relationship, but more importantly intimacy and connection.

From a psychobiological perspective looking into your partner's eyes is one of the most exciting things your brain can experience. Our brains love novelty and looking into your partner's eyes is a novel experience. Researchers report that when you both look into each other's eyes it allows you to regulate each other's nervous systems. This is because eye-gazing allows you both to anchor yourself in real-time to allow you to be present to each other. Your eyes are ever-changing and offer each of you something different each time.

Exercise:

Sit close together facing each other. You can sit on the floor or in chairs knee to knee. Look into each other's eyes. Do this for a period of time without speaking – at least five minutes and preferably about 15 minutes.

When you do this exercise you may feel uncomfortable, you may want to turn away, resist, laugh or even cry. Just notice any feelings or behaviours that arise, stay with the emotion and continue to gently look into your partners eyes. As you continue to do this you may notice that your breathing starts to slow down and you will both begin to feel quiet, relaxed and safe. This occurs because it is through focused eye attention that you both can regulate each other's emotions.

Relax, breathe and allow the experience to unfold. Notice what arises without judging it. Be open and curious, like a child experiencing something for the first time. You are showing your true self to your partner. To deepen your experience inhale and exhale together at the same time so that your breathing becomes synchronised.

Mindful body scan

This body scan is provided to you as a basic introduction to mindfulness. Mindfulness is important to your relationship, as it is a technique that when practised on a regular basis has the impact of reducing physical and emotional stress. As you know stress can impact your relationship in a number of ways and none of them are positive. The body scan takes approximately seven minutes and is designed for you to use on your own or together with your partner.

To download your free mindful body scan and other goodies please go to www.rewireyourelationship.com/resources

Body Sensory

This exercise is especially designed as a way to introduce more trust and safety into your relationship and will also build intimacy between the two of you. To benefit from this exercise it is best if you are naked or wearing underwear so that your skin is showing.

Exercise:

Before you begin:

Choose a time and place that works for both of you, where you won't be disturbed. Make the surroundings as pleasant as possible, ensure the room temperature is warm enough and you have soft lighting and aromas to enhance your experience.

Instead of expecting a specific outcome, take your time and enjoy the experience.

Beginning

You can either lie down or stand up for this exercise, whatever you both agree feels comfortable. Facing each other slowly and gently put your hand on their shoulders. While you continue to look at each other, describe to your partner what sensations you notice as your hand gently moves over their shoulders then down over their arms and then hands. For example, "I can feel that your skin is a little warm in this spot" or "I notice here it feels a little rough". Continue to move your hands over your partner's body in sections and describe to them what you feel. Take your time to pay attention to what you physically notice on your partner's body and describe only that to them. You are not describing your perceptions or ideas, only the actuality of what you have physically felt. When you have described as much of their body as possible it is your partners turn to do the same for you.

Exercise (continued):

Closing

When you have both described your bodies to each other talk to each other about how the exercise felt emotionally.

Practising this simple exercise increases the oxytocins in your brain that incline you to be close to your partner. It also reduces your partners' blood pressure and physiological stress levels. As with most things in life the more you practise something the easier it becomes. It may take a few practises before you begin to feel a greater sense of safety and security together. So ensure you practise often.

Mirror Movements

Listening to music you enjoy is another way to release dopamine in your brain. Movement and dancing with your partner will release dopamine as well as other health-related benefits. This form of movement is an energetic exercise that is designed to create fun novelty and rapport between the two of you.

Exercise:

Before you begin

Discuss which favourite pieces of music you would like to move to. I recommend something not too fast or slow paced. An idea is to choose a piece of music that is familiar or a favourite for both of you.

Decide who is going to be the leader and who is going to be the follower. After approximately 20 minutes you can swap.

Begin

Face each other. The leader begins to move their hands, legs and whole body any way they want to. The follower pays close attention and mirrors the leader's movements so you are both synchronised. The follower watches their partner's facial expressions while they are moving and also mirrors the expression their partner is using. Have fun with this experience and enjoy mirroring each other's movements and expressions. Notice when you both begin to synchronise, as you will start to know what movement your partner is going to do slightly before or exactly when they do it.

Exercise (continued):

Ending

After 20 minutes or so it's time to swap from leader to follower and continue in your dance moves until you notice that your behaviour becomes synchronised. You may choose to use different music or continue with the same. Again have fun with this exercise this is designed to help you build trust and safety with each other as well as injecting some light-heartedness into your relationship.

Mirroring is something that attuned couples often do with each other without their awareness.

When you first met your partner, you would have most likely mirrored their body language without being consciously aware of doing so. When you mirror your partner, whether it's their body language or facial expressions, the rapport you build sends an unconscious signal that you trust and understand each other. It is an excellent way to build trust and understanding quickly. If you want to re-establish a connection with your partner, pay attention to their posture, gestures, sitting position, tone of voice and talking pace and mirror it. Your partner will begin to feel more comfortable and secure as well as believing that you like them.

Love Visualisation

If your sex life has stalled lately or you have not felt any sexual inclination for your partner this simple practice can be helpful in recreating your desire again.

Intentions

First, you need to set a deliberate intention to develop the kind of sex life that you would like to have or enjoy. An intention is like a plan or an aim of something you would like to create. You can create this in your mind or write it down.

Self-Talk

You need to become acutely aware of your inner self-talk about sex and notice what you say to yourself or what you say to your partner about sex. Notice the language you use. Our minds are designed in a way that whatever we focus our thoughts on will be created. Simply put whatever we tell ourselves over and over is what we will create in our lives. If you are telling yourself that you are too tired or too stressed or it's too much hassle to bother with sex, then that is how you will feel and that is what you will create. Instead, change the way you speak to yourself and your partner about your sexual relationship.

Visualise

Imagine the sexual relationship that you desire. See that being played out in your mind. Visualise in as much detail as possible what is happening between you and your partner.

You will find the visualisation will be easier because you have already set the intention and started changing the way you think and talk about sex.

Hugging

Touch is one of the ways we communicate love, including foot rubs, back rubs, hair brushing or simply holding hands. Your brain releases a hormone during physical contact called oxytocin, often called the love drug. This is the same chemical that is released when you orgasm during sex. By using this natural biological boost in your brain, hugging will help you connect to your partner both physically and emotionally. After hugging you will feel a greater sense of closeness with each other. Hugging without expectation or hidden agendas also increases the likelihood of creating a physical sense of safety and security in your relationship.

You can hug your partner as often as you both like, as the more you hug the more relaxed and comfortable you will both be with physical contact. A great time to hug your partner is after you have been away from each other for a prolonged period and you have just come back together again. This can include coming home to each other after a day at work.

Exercise:

- Without talking, stand facing each other, looking into each other's eyes
- Wrap your arms around each other and hold each other
- Snuggle into shoulders or neck if preferred
- Notice your own and your partner's body softening and calming down
- Continue holding each other until you notice the stress and pressure leave your bodies.
- When ready to release the hugging, with arms around your partner look into their eyes again and begin to move slowly apart.

This exercise is a gentle way to reconnect with each other without any expectations and is especially helpful if you are not ready for a deeper level of intimacy. It can create a form of intimacy without words that may allow more talking intimacy in the future.

Yab-Yum Pose

You can practise this exercise either clothed or naked. Yab-Yum Pose is a traditional tantric pose used to physically connect with your partner. Traditionally tantric practices have been developed with male and female energy in mind, however this practice works equally as well with same sex couples. This is a very intimate way to connect with your partner.

One of you sits on the floor or bed cross-legged – traditionally this is the male partner. If you have any discomfort you can sit with your back facing the wall. The other partner (often the female) sits down on top of his legs facing him.

Put your arms around each other in an embrace and breathe slowly and fully together belly to belly. Continue breathing and slowly begin to focus your attention on your partner's face and eyes.

Continue gazing into each other's eyes, allowing whatever feelings you experience to arise. This assists with keeping your attention on the present moment which in turn allows you both to fully relax and experience all that you need or want to.

Synchronise your breathing and allow yourself to appreciate this special contact with each other and being connected in this way.

Move back to hugging your partner and begin to focus your attention on how your partner smells. Pay particular attention to the smell of their neck or hair or upper chest. Allow yourself to breathe in their scent as if that is the only aroma you notice.

Now gently make small circles with your hands on your partners back, head neck and hair. Focus all of your attention on your sense of touch noticing how it feels to be touched and to touch your partner's body.

After a while you may feel the desire to kiss your partner. Again allow yourself to kiss slowly so you can both savour the experience of kissing. Immerse yourself in the sensation of kissing. This exercise is a beautiful, intimate and intense way to begin making love with your partner.

Pillow Talk

Men and women have been having erotic fantasies since the dawn of time and research tells us that figure is between 95% to 98% of the population. Of course not everyone wants to act on their fantasies and some prefer to keep them as just that, a fantasy, but it can be of benefit for you to share some of them with your partner.

There are a number of different factors that influence what you fantasise about, including your attachment style. If you or your partner has an avoidant style you will tend to fantasise more about casual, non-emotional sex. Partners with an ambivalent style are more likely to fantasise about pleasing their partner. And the partners who have a secure attachment style are most likely to fantasise about romantic, loving sex. Other factors that contribute to what you fantasise about are your hormones, age, personality, past sexual experiences, relationship length and satisfaction level.

Sexual fantasies have been found to improve your relationship as long as it is your partner you are fantasising about. Your

partner loves to see you turned on and one of the ways to increase your sexual arousal is through fantasies. When you fantasise about your partner it increases your desire for them and guides you into showing them more affection love and support. When you understand that you are essentially a biological being in that your sexual desire is influenced by chemical releases in your brain, it helps in reducing any shame and insecurity you may feel. Incorporating fantasies into your sex life has been found to increase your relationship satisfaction especially if you find you are sexually inhibited.

Exercise:

Before you begin

This part is simply to begin to open the topic about sharing some of your thoughts not necessarily enacting on any of them.

Find a time to gently introduce the topic of things that turn you on. You can ask your partner the question "How can we explore some of the things that turn us on?" or "Are you open to talking about what we enjoy in bed?". One simple way to begin is to ask your partner to tell you what they enjoy you doing to them, for example "What is it I do to you that you really like?" or "What's the favourite thing we do in bed together?". Or you could tell your partner, "I loved it when you started kissing me from behind".

Exercise (continued):

This can then lead to both of you sharing with each other about some of the things you both find sexually exciting.

Beginning

Once you both know some of the things that turn you on, decide between you who is going to create a fantasy including the two of you. Once you've decided, you can face each other to listen, or you can ask your partner to lie behind you and softly whisper the fantasy into your ear. It's really important to give gentle feedback to your partner whilst listening. Even though you have a shared agreement about what you both enjoy sexually, feedback helps guide your partner along the way. If you find you are becoming sexually aroused, you can incorporate your ideas into the fantasy, for example "I want to…" or "And then this happened".

Closing

Talk to each other about what it felt like to listen to what each of you were saying, most importantly which parts of the fantasy you enjoyed the most. If you find that you gradually moved into making love or having sex then clearly something worked. Even if that did happen, find the time afterward to talk to each other about what aspects you enjoyed the most.

Above all have fun with this.

A Novel Idea...

After all the chemical cocktails and excitement your brain produces in the attraction phase of your relationship you may feel disappointed that your fire and energy for each other has started to wane. This is very natural as you move into the attachment phase of your relationship.

Nothing gets your passion and intensity happening for each other more than having sex. Having sex reactivates those love neurotransmitters oxytocin and dopamine. Your feeling intensity will increase with orgasmic sex and frequency of sex. Yes having regular sex does wonders for relationship satisfaction and well-being. And don't rush it. Make love passionately and slowly.

Feel the skin of your partner. Admire each other's bodies and tell each other. Pause for a second and ask yourself how do I feel right now in this moment. Ask your partner how do you feel right now this moment. Whatever the answer there is no judgment this is just to tune into yourself and each other.

Try something new, put your brave boots on and become sexually adventurous. It really does not matter what you do that is different as long as it is just that DIFFERENT. Just doing something novel will raise your dopamine levels.

Ensure you orgasm, as experiencing an orgasm helps you release some of that oxytocin so you can keep that really intimate cuddly bonding feeling together. If you don't know what brings you to orgasm find out! Include your partner in your discovery it will be much more fun.

If you want to keep that passion burning you need to work at stoking the fires of your neurotransmitters.

PART SIX

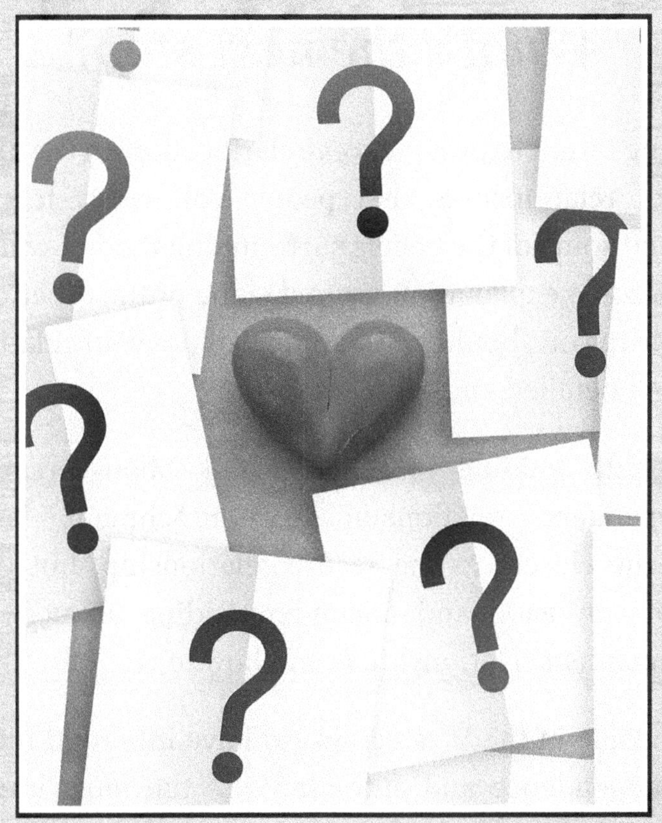

What's the Next Step?

PART SIX

What's the next step?

In closing I want to provide some clarification on the different styles of relationships that people commonly talk about today and some of the beliefs surrounding them. I will briefly provide some explanation around some of the other options available to you should you want to explore your relationship in a more detailed and intimate way.

In the fifth guiding principle, I talk about creating an interdependent relationship. In attachment language this is the closest to the secure relationship, but there is a lot of confusion and misunderstanding about what an interdependent relationship is and how to work toward it.

Many people in the Western world have inherited the belief that independence and autonomy are the most important qualities in an individual. Partners carry this attitude into their relationships and believe that each person should be independent of the other and not expect to be protected or cared for. We have all heard the statement, 'that's your problem not mine'. This belief partly stemmed from psychologists in the early 1970s who promoted the individualistic ideals of

separateness within relationships – separateness or being emotionally apart from each other was seen as being strong, and being strong was linked to survival.

Our culture today believes being independent of each other as a couple is the relationship goal to aspire to. Couples often talk with pride about how their partner does their thing and they do theirs, but at the same time struggle to understand why behaving in this way does not create the emotional closeness they desire or even bring them happiness with each other. This is because, contrary to what we have previously been taught, a relationship is not two separate people doing their own thing or bumping up against each other occasionally. This idea is no longer valid in a country where on average it only takes eight and a half years for a married couple to separate, and it's only twelve years in total till divorce (ABS 2015).

Part of what feeds the preference of relationship independence and isolation is the dread of being in a relationship that is in opposition to that. On this end of the spectrum we hear of relationships that are co-dependent. The idea of co-dependency or 'I will do everything for you but it will be at the expense of myself', came out of research into alcoholism in the 1980s that examined a person's compulsive inclination to be in relationships with chemically dependent partners – a person was considered co-dependent if they were in love with or married to an alcoholic, or had one or more alcoholic parents or grandparents.

The term then became widely used to describe any form of relationship where addictive behaviours were present and was quickly applied to relationships in general. For many years co-dependency in a relationship was misinterpreted to represent a couple that was weak, clingy, needy and even emotionally unwell and by default it was viewed as a relationship to be ashamed of. Thirty years later, the term co-dependency has become misrepresented from its original meaning. This is so much the case that many therapists refrain from using it in clinical settings. Today the term co-dependency is used more generally to apply to people who have a pattern of relationships where one person focuses on the needs and behaviours of others more than their own. Essentially people who are co-dependent become so preoccupied and focused on the needs of others that they neglect their own needs. You may have noticed that this way of relating is closest to the anxious ambivalent attachment style. And of course the isolating-independent relationship is very similar to how an anxious-avoidant person relates to their partner.

This brings us to the type of relationship that this book is based on helping you achieve, an interdependent relationship. Although we may like to believe as a society that we live quite independently, in fact we actually operate interdependently.

We depend on each other for many things for example, having running water and electricity, supermarkets, and of course our ever-increasing technology, just to name a few.

Ironically the interdependent couple are able to function independently of each other but are both committed to their relationship and at the same time depend on each other. The relationship has its own life, like the garden that the couple tends to so that it can develop and blossom fully. The couple depend upon each other to fill their emotional needs including sexual and social, as well as friendship, communication, nurturing, appreciation, learning, love, and touch. Another important component in an interdependent relationship is a strong sense of self or self-esteem, which allows the couple to honour each other's differences as well as each other's separateness. The closer your relationship, the more you're interconnected. This is the secure base relationship that I spoke about earlier as it is a safe way of relating because each person is involved in the other person's life without sacrificing each other or individual values.

Moving Forward with Your Relationship

People are often unsure of where to go or what to do when they first think about getting some assistance with their relationship. Often when couples actually make the decision to 'see someone', it's when they have been struggling for a long time and feel immense pressure to get it fixed now, but don't know who to see or how to see them. If they have trusted friends they may ask them or perhaps check out social media sites. Many people do their own research by scrolling through numerous websites trying to find the right fit for them before they make that call. Still others will ask their local doctor to refer them.

It's not really surprising people are uncertain, as today there are many different terms used to describe the value of talking through your emotional problems – couples treatment, psychotherapy, relationship coaching or marriage counselling, to name just a few. Then of course there are a myriad of techniques theories and approaches provided by many different professionals that the whole process can sometimes be downright mystifying. All of this confusion increases the likelihood that people will delay making that first appointment and getting the help they need. Combine all of the above with Australian's reluctance to seek help and you can see why many couples tend to leave it till the last moment.

I want to briefly provide a way forward should you feel that after reading this book you would benefit from seeing a couples therapist.

Psychology is traditionally an approach that works with an individual, so the framework is typically to assist the

individual. Psychologists are experts in human behaviour and use evidence-based strategies and interventions to help people overcome challenges and improve their performance. They are university trained for many years to use scientific methods to study the factors that influence the way that people think, feel and learn. Many psychologists work directly with those experiencing difficulties, such as mental health disorders including anxiety and depression. Their focus is not typically on the past but better functioning for their clients now and in the future. Many psychologists specialise in particular areas, including eating disorders, substance abuse, parenting problems and relationship difficulties, to name a few. Some psychologists are trained in different theories of psychotherapy and may also offer this depending on what is required. Psychotherapy is an approach that includes amongst other things, exploring a couple's past including their family of origin and patterns of behaviour. Together with the therapist the couple can look at unconscious meanings and motivations that they are bringing into their relationship.

Some people in a relationship choose to see a therapist on their own as they may believe that the problem lies with them alone. Whilst that may be partially true, when you are a couple whatever you are feeling or however you are behaving affects your partner and vice versa, because remember you are tied together. Even if you believe you are shielding your partner from worries or concerns, your partner will still be affected, which in turn has repercussions for you.

Couples therapy can be more intense than individual therapy, as you are both there together and it's not as easy to hide from your relationship dynamic with your partner. With the therapist you are both invited to co-create the process of change. However the therapist is there to encourage you to start talking about whatever is causing you concern or to perhaps work out what some of those issues are for you. Some couples therapists focus on communication styles and how to talk differently to your partner – as you will have now realised, changing the way you talk to your partner will make a significant difference to your relationship. Couples therapy can be incredibly helpful and a great relief for the both of you to finally say some of those things that you have long held inside.

Overall, if you don't have a recommendation, do some research, look for therapists that you believe will offer you what you are looking for and then call them up and talk to them. Ask them to explain how they will work with you what is their approach. Listen to their tone of voice when they are talking and tune into how you feel when you are listening to them. When it comes down to it, finding the 'right' therapist is really about getting the best fit for you as a couple. It is essential that you feel rapport between you and your therapist and you believe they understand both of you and what you are

going through. Because therapists are human too they are as different as you are and all have different styles, approaches, training and expertise.

If after a few sessions it doesn't feel right for the both of you it's absolutely fine to say that to your therapist and look for someone else and try again. After all it's your relationship and its worth working on.

Author's Final Word

Now that you have read this book you will realise that there is no such thing as a perfect relationship. We are human beings and by default we are imperfect, which, by the way, is the beauty of us. Try as you might to change your partner most of what you are trying to change is their individual attachment style which, as you now know, is pretty much hard-wired. If you accept and work together with whatever styles you are you give yourselves a greater chance of creating your own unique secure base relationship. But also know that you will make mistakes and maybe sometimes lots of them. Accept who you are warts and all; remember you have been given a particular template that you are trying to learn to work with as does your partner. Don't be too hard on yourself or emotionally beat yourself up. Be kind to yourself, show compassion to yourself and your partner. Understand and accept you are most likely doing the best you can and if you don't think you are then do something different. There's always another chance at making your relationship expand grow and develop.

My wish for you is to have a happier healthier and more attached relationship. My hope is that the content in this book has gone some way toward helping you create your own unique relationship attachment style, your secure base relationship.

An ode to your interdependent relationship

Here is the deepest secret nobody knows
I carry your heart with me (I carry it in
my heart) I am never without it (anywhere
I go you go, my dear; and whatever is done
by only me is your doing, my darling)
I fear no fate (for you are my fate, my sweet)
I want no world (for beautiful you are my world, my true)
and it's you are whatever a moon has always meant
and whatever a sun will always sing is you
here is the deepest secret nobody knows
(here is the root of the root and the bud of the bud
and the sky of the sky of a tree called life; which grows
higher than the soul can hope or mind can hide)
and this is the wonder that's keeping the stars apart
I carry your heart (I carry it in my heart)

E. E. Cummings

About the Author

Jacqui Christie

Jacqui is an author, clinical psychologist, family violence specialist, relationship expert, and public speaker.

With more than 20 years of experience mediating family disputes and working with men who were violent, abusive, or controlling in their relationships, Jacqui enjoys helping men and women empower themselves. During her career she has counselled, coached, trained, and empowered thousands of people from all walks of life, including CEOs of major corporations, entrepreneurs, blue-collar workers, models, and actors.

In addition to speaking about family violence and women's personal development at events and seminars, she has been featured as a relationship expert in *Cleo Magazine*, *Women's Health Magazine*, *Girlfriend Magazine*, and on several television shows.

Jacqui's formal training includes a master's degree in psychology and additional clinical psychology study to

earn her clinical registration. She is also an accredited Psychobiological Approach to Couples Therapy (PACT) Level I Therapist, a qualified Family Law Court Mediator, and a Clinical Hypnotist. She is proud to have survived a significant childhood trauma to become the first person in her family to attend university. Jacqui also takes pride in having completed her education while also being a wife and raising two children.

Jacqui has also enjoyed an acting career, having made appearances in live theatre, in the television shows including *Prisoner*, *The Sullivans*, and *Skyways*, as well as in the movie *Water Under the Bridge*. Her professional associations include the Australian Psychological Association, the College of Counselling Psychologists, the Psychology Board of Australia, and World Vision.

She has travelled and worked throughout Scotland, England, Wales, Italy, France, Switzerland, Germany, Austria, Netherlands, Spain, Belgium, the United States of America, Singapore, Malaysia and Yemen.

Jacqui Christie is the author of *Rewire Your Relationship* and lives in Victoria, Australia.

RECOMMENDED

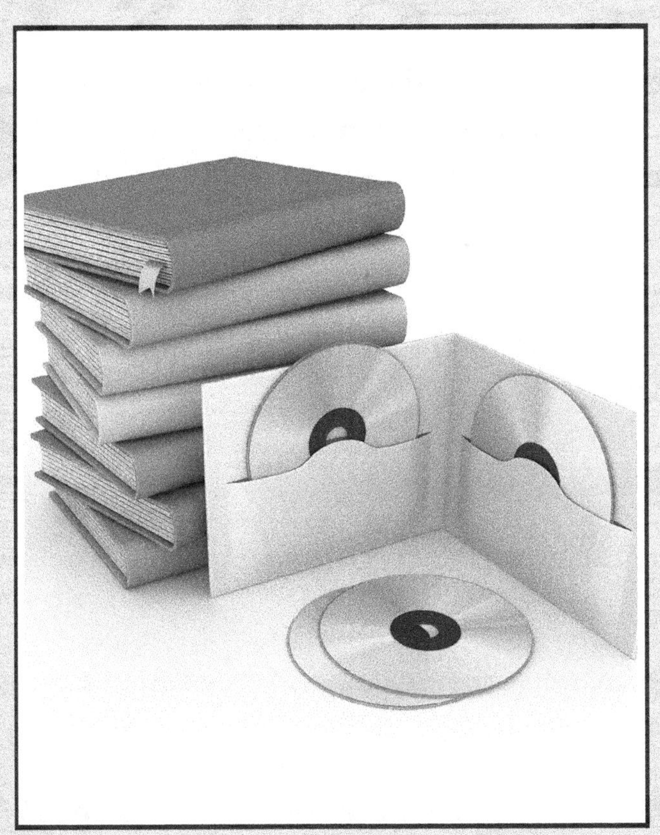

RESOURCES

Recommended Resources

These are just a few of the books and audio I recommend. I hope you gain as much as I have from reading and listening to these greats in my field.

Poetry

E. E. Cummings (1954) *100 Selected Poems* Grove Press, Inc. New York

Books

Harville Hendrix (1988). *Getting the Love You Want: A Guide for Couples*

David Schnarch (1997). *Passionate Marriage: Keeping Love and Intimacy Alive in Committed Relationships.*

John Gottman and Nan Silver (2015). *The Seven Principles for Making Marriage Work: A practical guide from the nation's foremost relationship expert*

Marion Solomon and Stan Tatkin (2011). *Love and War in Intimate Relationships: Connection, disconnection and mutual regulation in couple therapy.*

Stan Tatkin (2014). *Wired for Love: How understanding your partner's brain and attachment style can help you defuse conflict and build a secure relationship.*

Amir Levine and Rachael Heller (2010). *Attached: The new science of adult attachment and how it can help you find and keep love.*

Audio Series

Stan Tatkin. (2013). *Your Brain on Love: The Neurobiology of Healthy Relationships* Audio CD – Audiobook

Want A Dynamic Health And Relationship Speaker Or Trainer At Your Next Conference?

❤ JACQUI CHRISTIE ❤

Speaker Trainer and Facilitator in motivational mindset and positive transformative relationships.

Jacqui Christie has over 23-years-experience in the private and community sectors in coaching and assisting people with their relationships. From the boardroom to the bedroom Jacqui understands human behaviour and why people behave the way they do. She will take your participants through an innovative process of understanding themselves to ensure only the best possible outcomes.

Whether you are looking to motivate your teams, increase staff output, find more balance, reduce stress or improve customer relations. Jacqui's principles when put into practice will create permanent change in your participant's relationships and therefore in the day to day operations of your company.

Presentation Formats

Keynote

This engaging and thought provoking program will leave your conference or meeting participants energised and excited about the material they have just learnt. We guarantee your participants will see themselves and others in a new light and understand the unconscious motivations in all their relationships.

Full Day or Half Day workshops

This is a 4 to 8 hour tailored program to your individual organisation. The workshops are focussed on your organisations outcomes and objectives and utilises exercises, activities and group experiences. This allows for a deeper understanding of the material to achieve personal growth among participants. Manual with key learning tools included.

More details on our website www.RewireYouRelationship.com

Retreats

Coming Soon exclusive small group couples retreats. You and your partner will learn new skills for deepening your connection to each other learn how to manage conflicts and strengthen your communication.

More details on our website www.RewireYouRelationship.com

Imagine what you could accomplish working with your own Personal Relationship Coach

Jacqui offers intimate couples coaching, through face to face and online coaching programs. Her professional expertise allows you and your partner the space and time to discover what's blocking you from achieving the relationship you both deserve. Jacqui will dedicate her time to your relationship and provide you with the tools and techniques to rediscover each other developed from over 23-years-experience in helping couples just like you. If you are seeking personalised special attention while enhancing and restoring your relationship then this is definitely the program for you.

For a confidential discussion about how Jacqui can assist you in creating the relationship you have always dreamt of, please go to:

www.RewireYouRelationship.com

References

I could not have written this book without the incredible research from the people below.

Acevedo, B.P., Aron, A., Fisher, H.E., & Brown, L.L (2011) Neural correlates of long-term intense romantic Love. *Social Cognitive and Affective Neuroscience* 2012 Feb;7 (2):145-59 doi: 10.1093/scan/nsq092 Epub 2011 Jan 5

Bowlby, J. (1969/1982). *Attachment: Attachment and Loss* (Vol. 1). New York: Basic Books.

Bowlby, J. (1980). *Loss: Sadness and Depression*, Vol. 3. New York, NY: Basic Books.

Bowlby, J. (1988). *A Secure Base: Parent-Child Attachment and Healthy Human Development.* Routledge, London

Brown, N. M., & Amatea, E. S. (2000). *Love and Intimate Relationships: Journeys of the heart.* Brunner/Mazel, Philadelphia PA

Campbell, L., Simpson, J. A., Boldry, J., & Kashy, D. A. (2005). Perceptions of conflict and support in romantic relationships: The role of attachment anxiety. *Journal of Personality and Social Psychology, 88*, 510-531

Cassidy, J & Shaver P (Eds) (2016). *Handbook of Attachment: Theory, Research, and Clinical Applications Third Edition* New York NY: Guildford Press

Cummings, E. M., & Davies, P. T. (2010). *Marital conflict and children: An emotional security perspective.* New York, NY: Guilford Press.

Demasio, A. R (1994) *Descartes Error: Emotion reason and the human brain* Avon Books

Eliot, A. J., & Reis, H.T (2003). Attachment and Exploration in Adulthood. *Journal of Personality and Social Psychology 2003, Vol. 85, No. 2, 317–331*

Feeney, B.C., & Van Vleet, M. (2010). Growing through attachment: The interplay of attachment and exploration in adulthood. *Journal of Social and Personal Relationships*, 27, 226-234.

Feeney, B. C., & Thrush, R. L. (2010). Relationship influences on exploration in adulthood: The characteristics and function of a secure base. *Journal of Personality and Social Psychology,* 98, 57-76

Fraley, R. C., Waller, N. G., & Brennan, K. A. (2000). An item-response theory analysis of self-report measures of adult attachment. *Journal of Personality and Social Psychology*, *78*, 350-365

Fraley R,C (2010). A Brief Overview of Adult Attachment Theory and Research. Retrieved from <internal.psychology.illinois.edu/~rcfraley/attachment.htm>

Gottman, J. M., & Silver, N (1999). How I predict divorce," in *The Seven Principles for Making Marriages Work.* New York: Three Rivers Press Random House, Inc.

Gottman, J. M., & Silver, N (1999/2015). *The Seven Principles for Making Marriages Work.* A Practical Guide from the Country's Foremost Relationship Expert. New York: Harmony Books

Shaver, P & Mikulincer, M (2007). Adult attachment strategies and the regulation of emotion in Handbook of Emotion Regulation (pg 446- 465) In J. J. Gross (Ed.), *Handbook of emotion regulation* (pp. 446-465). New York: Guilford Press.

Hazan, C., & Shaver, P. (1987). Romantic love conceptualized as an attachment process. *Journal of Personality and Social Psychology,* 52(3), 511-524.

Hazan, C., & Shaver, P.R (1990). Love and work: An attachment-theoretical perspective. *Journal of Personality and Social Psychology,* Vol 59(2), pp 270-280 http://dx.doi.org/10.1037/0022-3514.59.2.270

Hendrix, H (1988) *Getting the love you want: A guide for couples.* Melbourne: Schwartz and Wilkinson.

Kobak, R., & Duemmler, S. (1994). Attachment and conversation: A discourse analysis of goal-corrected partnerships. Chapter for D. Perlman and K. Bartholomew (Eds.), *Advances in the study of personal relationships, Vol. 5,* (pp. 121-149). London: Jessica Kingsley Publishers.

Lancer, D. (2014) *Conquering Shame and Codependency: 8 Steps to Freeing the True You.* Minnesota: Hazeldene Publishing

Lanciano & Zammuner (2014) Individual Differences in Work-Related Well-Being: The Role of Attachment Style, *Europe's Journal of Psychology,* Vol 10, No 4

LeDoux, J (1996) *The Emotional Brain: The Mysterious Underpinnings of Emotional Life.* New York: Simon and Shuster.

Levine, A., Heller, R,S.F. (2010) Attached. The new science of adult attachment and how it can help you find and keep love. New York: Jeremy P. Tarcher/ Penguin.

Mikulincer, M., Dolev, T., & Shaver, P. R. (2004). Attachment-Related Strategies During Thought Suppression: Ironic Rebounds and Vulnerable Self-Representations. *Journal of Personality and Social Psychology,* 87(6), 940-956.

Markman, H. J., Stanley, S. M., Jenkins. N. H., Petrella, J. N.,Wadsworth, M. E.(2006). Preventive Education: Distinctives and Directions *Journal of Cognitive Psychotherapy*: An International Quarterly Volume 20, Number 4

Mikulincer, M., & Shaver, P. R. (2005). *Attachment theory and emotions in close relationships*: Exploring the attachment-related dynamics of emotional reactions to relational events. Personal Relationships, 12, 149-168

Mikulincer, M., & Shaver, P. R. (2007). *Attachment in adulthood: Structure, dynamics, and change.* New York, NY US: Guilford Press.

Moullin, S., Waldfogel, J & Washbrook, E. (2014 March) Baby Bonds. Parenting Attachment and a Secure Base for Children. London: The Sutton Trust. Copy at www.suttontrust.com/wp-content/uploads/2014/03/baby-bonds-final.pdf

Paré, D (2003) Role of the basolateral amygdala in memory consolidation. *Progress in Neurobiology* 70, 409–420

Pearce, C. (2009). A Short Introduction to Attachment and Attachment Disorder. London: Jessica Kingsley Publishers.

Schore, A.N. (1994). *Affect regulation and the origin of the self:* The neurobiology of emotional development. Mahwah, NJ: Erlbaum

Siegel, D.(1999) *The Developing Mind*, New York: Guildford Press.

Solomon, M., Tatkin, S (2011). *Love and War in Intimate Relationships.* Connection, Disconnection and mutual regulation in couple therapy. New York: W.W. Norton & Company, Inc.

Stanley, S., Trathen, D., McCain, S., & Bryan, M. (2014). A Lasting Promise. San Francisco: Wiley and Sons, Inc.

Tatkin, S (2003). *Marital Therapy and the Psychobiology of Turning Toward and Turning Away.* Part 1. The Therapist, 15, 75-78.

Tatkin, S(2014). Wired for Love. How understanding your partner's brain and attachment style can help you defuse conflict and build a secure relationship

Tessina, T. B (2010). *How To Be a Couple and Still Be Free* ISBN #1-56414-549-2

Tessina, T. B (2010). *The Unofficial Guide to Dating Again* (Wiley) ISBN#0-02-862454-8

Treboux, D., Crowell, J. A., & Waters, E. (2004). When 'New' Meets 'Old': Configurations of Adult Attachment Representations and Their Implications for Marital Functioning. *Developmental Psychology*, 40(2), 295-314.

Thich.,N.,H., Kornfield. J., Kingston, M., Laity, A., Reed, C., Ellsberg, P.M., Halifax, J., Batchelor, S.,& Steindl-Rast, D.(1993) *For a Future to Be Possible: Commentaries on the Five Wonderful Precepts.* Parallax Press, PO Box 7355, Berkeley, CA 94707

Waters, E., Merrick, S., Treboux, D., Crowell, J., & Albersheim, L. (2000). Attachment security in infancy and early adulthood: A twenty-year longitudinal study. *Child Development*, 71(3), 684-689.

www.ingramcontent.com/pod-product-compliance
Lightning Source LLC
Chambersburg PA
CBHW072004090426
42740CB00011B/2081

* 9 7 8 1 9 2 5 2 8 8 1 2 4 *